EXPERIENCING ASTRAL TRAVEL
An 8 Week Course

What others are saying about this course:

"... It shows us how advantaged we are here - VM Beelzebub is a superb communicator, being able to convey vastly abstruse information with seemingly relative ease. It makes a wonderful change and it breaks with tradition."

Chris

"I'm so ecstatic! I've just discovered what I can do. It's as if I'm seeing, for the first time EVER, my capabilities as a human being. And how impressive it is to go into the Astral and manifest at an instant, no less than an instant. I projected completely consciously."

Gina

"Throughout my experience I have seen a lot of support for the people attending these courses. I feel that this place (the website) is a blessing for anyone willing to take that step forward to see the deeper side of yourself."

Michael, Melbourne, Australia

"I really think that this course can let all people achieve Astral Travel and provides essential information. It is as detailed as it can get."

Janet, Texas, USA

"After taking the course I have totally changed the way I view the world, life and everything around me, and inside me."

aXe, Australia

"I would like to develop what I know is possible. Astral Travel works, folks..."

Lucius Swag, California, USA

"I feel that (these courses) are not only unique, but if properly used, they could change mankind and its way of thinking."

Yama

"There is really no comparison between what is read and what is experienced, so I urge you to persist and have faith. Something that I have found is the alluring quality of the Astral - it's like you can FEEL the timelessness and the wealth of knowledge that resides there. It is truly amazing."

Chris

"I just wanted to say, thank you! Without guidance from you, I would have never been able to experience the Astral. Thanks again!

Chrisalyne, Illinois, USA

"These tools should be taught in the schools. Congratulations for helping people be more aware, so we can have a better world!"

Pina, Montreal, Canada

"Thank you very very much for opening this window of opportunity to souls that want to know the truth."

Roaddog Wylie J., Ohio, USA

"Tell the world about the Astral World and may we all grow in experience and visit the Angels in the heavenly realms!"

Scott Hearyman, Arizona, USA

"Thanks for the course, I really needed it. It is good to find people who are not scared to share their knowledge."

Pablo Fallas, San Jose, Costa Rica

The above are unprompted comments from students that have taken this course online.

EXPERIENCING ASTRAL TRAVEL
An 8 Week Course

V.M. Beelzebub

IMPORTANT NOTICE

This publication is intended to provide helpful and informative material on the subjects addressed herein and is purchased with the understanding that the author and publisher are not engaged in rendering professional advice or services to the individual reader.

The information contained in this book is not intended as a substitute for consulting with a health care professional. If you are suffering any medical condition, we encourage you to consult with a medical professional.

The accuracy and completeness of the information provided herein and the advice stated herein is not guaranteed or warranted to produce any particular results and the advice and strategies provided may not be suitable for every individual.

The author and the publisher disclaim any liability for loss, injury, or damages resulting directly or indirectly from the use or application of any of the contents of this book including any loss or injury resulting directly or indirectly from the negligence of the author or publisher. Any application of the material set forth in the following pages is at the readers discretion and is his or her sole responsibility.

All rights reserved. No part of this book may be reproduced or transmitted in any form or by any means, electronic or mechanical, including photocopying, recording, or by any information storage and retrieval system - except by a reviewer who may quote brief passages in a review to be printed in magazine, newspaper, or on the Web - without permission in writting from the copyright holder.

© Mark Pritchard

Absolute Publishing LLC
PMB #327, 39270 Paseo Padre Pkwy.,
Fremont, CA 94538-1616, USA
www.absolutepublishing.net

First edition: April 2003
ISBN: 0-9740560-0-6

Cover designed by Patricia Atkinson

Printed in Canada

Foreword

As a young teenager I first came across the notion of Astral Travel in a fiction novel which filled my mind with awe and wonder about the possibilities of flying, meeting strange and powerful people and exploring worlds which at that time only existed in my imagination. Although I was thrilled by the possible adventures, the novel also made me terrified about not being able to get back into my body, being terrorized by sadistic entities and remaining stuck in another realm. Even into my adult life, this novel and its story remained in the back of my mind, but I never took the possibilities of Astral travel as being something I could seriously do, let alone learn from and develop greater understanding about my life and its purpose.

A few years ago, I received a leaflet in my mailbox advertising an Astral Travel Course and, even though I was still a bit anxious about the legitimacy and safety of the idea, I thought to myself, "It is now or never, just find out what it's about". You can imagine my great surprise and shock when I found myself beginning to experience the sensations associated with the "splitting" of the bodies after trying just the first Astral practice exercise. With further encouragement and investigation guided by the author of this book, V.M. Beelzebub, I found myself experiencing the unimaginable, traveling to faraway places, seeing wondrous things, given specific details of learning about myself which I could improve and meeting different Astral beings

I can categorically say that knowledge and verification of the Astral dimension has changed my life and continues to shape how I want to live it. It was not that long ago that I was suffering from a great deal of anxiety about my life, not knowing what it is for, how I can have an impact in shaping its course and helping those around me in similar situations. And it's not as though I had any reason for feeling these worries. I come from a very stable family, live in a comfortable home in a very safe country with a fantastic job as a radio broadcaster on the National Youth Network JJJ. Something was definitely missing though and I was lucky enough to have found the guidance to help me look for the path of spiritual fulfillment.

Achieving greater clarity and sustained experiences in the Astral is now a constant goal I'm working toward, the reverse of that fear of not being able to come back to the physical body. Being able to travel and experience the Astral has given me great strength to broaden and continue my search to understand myself and the way of the forces which govern life.

In that context, why waste time wondering like I did? I have been extremely privileged to have been instructed by V.M. Beelzebub, a person who has achieved an exceptional level of understanding and knowledge about the Astral. He gave me the tools to investigate for myself and guided me through all the doubts and fears and through his teachings I have gained a true focus in life. I'd wholeheartedly encourage you to take this book, read its wisdom and try it for yourself.

Happy Astral Travels!

Caroline Tran
Radio Broadcaster, Triple J

Preface by the Author

This book will take you step by step along the techniques and exercises, which will allow you to experience Astral travel; it will explain what the Astral world is and what you can do when you go there. It also explains what dreams are, what their relationship with Astral travel is and how you can use them to improve your daily life. The book is an initial guidance to get you off to a good start in your Astral Travels and forms a sound basis for further exploration.

It is compiled from the Astral Travel course that I run on the Internet and in study centres where it is taught to live groups. It has been very successful in terms of getting people to actually experience the Astral plane, so its contents are very much already tried and tested.

I have been teaching Astral projection techniques in person for around thirteen years and on the internet for about three years. I wasn't born with the ability to Astral project like some people, so I had to learn how to do it and, sometimes with great struggles, to overcome many obstacles until the techniques succeeded. This has allowed me to gather techniques that work and to be able to pass on solutions to overcome the most common difficulties encountered.

I have learned so much from the Astral plane and from other higher and lower planes that are beyond the scope of this book. But I remember many happy and exciting times when I first learned to project, a group of us would get together at weekends and spend the whole time practicing for the Astral, there were quite a few competent projectors amongst us and at least one person would get out of their body at every attempt we made. It was great to lie down as a group and to get up and see someone else already out. The days and nights became magical; I hope that this book will bring that magic into people's lives.

This book has been ready for release for about a year now, but it was held up due to one thing or another, finally it's here and I hope it will enable many more people to explore into the multi-dimensional reality of life.

You can try this course by following the book alone, but I recommend that you use it in conjunction with the course that I have online or in study centres. When you go to try to Astral Travel, you will be more successful if you make up your mind to follow what is written in this book as a complete course rather than to just read it through or to skim through bits of it at random and then to practice the exercises from it here and there. That is because the different exercises and techniques all follow on from one another, so for getting the best results they should be practiced in the order and in the 8 week timeframe that I give in the book.

This timeframe will give you enough time to experience something of the Astral; the more dedicated and disciplined you are towards it the more likely you are to have success.

This course is not about experiencing all aspects of the Astral plane and the esoteric worlds, it is about learning and exploring the techniques for Astral travel, it will enable you to get there and will give you most of what you need to travel out of the body. But to really explore that plane fully you need much more information than this book can provide. For this reason, I run other courses, which explain more fully, what is going on in the Astral world and in the human psyche. You will really need these other courses if you want to explore the Astral because there is so much going on there.

Anyone can learn to project, but it is quite another thing to know how to make best use of time spent in the Astral plane. For that, you have to know about the secret esoteric world and what the human psyche consists of, then you will really use your Astral journeys fruitfully and will have the chance to become a competent esotericist. Without this knowledge, you will only be able to gain incipient, basic information and will be trying to make sense of the unknown without the ability to do so.

To get started and to learn to experience the Astral world, this book will be a valuable tool. If you practice the exercises properly you will discover a lot about life and it will amaze you, but when you do you will also find that you have a whole lot more to discover. We are alive in the three dimensional world for just a short time, but we exist in eternity; it is there to be explored.

Mark Pritchard
(V.M. Beelzebub)

Contents

Foreword ix
Preface by the Author xi

Week 1
An Introduction to Dreams and Astral Travel
Introduction to the Astral Course 2
Dreams 3
The Astral Plane 5
Fear 8
There is no Danger 8
Will Power for Astral Projection 9
Week 1 Exercises 9
Questions and Answers 12

Week 2
How to Astral Project
Astral Projection 28
Establishing the Foundation for Astral Travel 28
The Problem of the Chattering Mind 29
Week 2 Exercises 31
How to Astral Project 32
Summary of Week 2 Exercises 38
Questions and Answers 39

Week 3
Waking Up in Dreams
Waking Up in Dreams 52
The Importance of Awareness 54
Week 3 Exercises 55
Questions and Answers 57

Week 4
Mantras for Astral Projection
Mantras for Astral Projection 66
Pronouncing the Mantras 66
Projecting with the Mantras 69
Week 4 Exercises 70
Questions and Answers 72

Week 5
Concentration
Concentration 80
Being Aware of What You Are Doing 80
Sitting Exercises 81
Problems with Falling Asleep 82
Using Breaks in the Nights Sleep to Increase
the Chances of Projection 82
Week 5 Exercises 83
Questions and Answers 85

Week 6
Dealing with Negative Entities
Negative Entities 90
Conjurations 92
Week 6 Exercises 97
Questions and Answers 98

Week 7
Astral and Dream Experiences
Using Intuition 110
Symbols in the Astral 111
What to Do in the Astral 112
Travelling 113
Week 7 Exercises 114
Questions and Answers 118

Supplementary Topics
General Dream Symbols 122
The Meaning of Numbers 134

Week 8
Overcoming Obstacles
Problems with Laziness 142
Being Disheartened 143
Problems with Pain When Doing Exercises 144
Lack of the Ability to Concentrate 145
Summary of the Course Exercises 146
Final Exercise of the Course 147
Conclusion 148

Where to go from Here
Planning the Exercises and your Astral Strategy 151
Getting into a Mode of Practicing 152
Dedication and Discipline 152

Index 155

Week 1

An Introduction to Dreams and Astral Travel

INTRODUCTION TO THE ASTRAL COURSE

This is the first of the weekly topics, there are eight weekly topics in all and each contains reading material followed by exercises for you to try at home daily. The course is written from my experience of the Astral world and the exercises I have found to be the most effective ones for getting there. It obviously does not contain everything that I have gone through in that dimension, but it lays the foundation for solid Astral experiences for those who wish to take it up.

This course will explain what the Astral is and what dreams are. It will tackle the basics of going into the Astral, laying the foundations for the real experience and for getting results in the exercises. This first topic gives a broad outline of dreams and the Astral, we will be focusing more upon the techniques to get there in the following topics. It is an intensive course so you need to do the exercises as best as you can so that you get results.

The Astral is one of two planes of the fifth dimension; it is the place where dreams occur, where mystical teachings are given and where the deceased go. It is more than that though because it is a complete dimension of life, waiting to be explored. It is possible to go there consciously and this course will teach you how. It is something real, not a figment of the imagination, but another place that exists and with the techniques on this course you can prove it.

Along with our other courses, it will give you the proven techniques to not only go into the Astral, but also to get real esoteric knowledge. Visiting the Astral plane can change your whole view of life. You can fly and have a bit of experience here and there but the aim is to do something worthwhile, which is to receive esoteric knowledge. With this in mind, you can meet spiritual beings in the Astral, discover secret knowledge, learn about yourself, see where your spiritual obstacles and your inner defects are, learn hidden wisdom about death, the process of awakening, get premonitions of the future, receive guidance, discover the purpose of life, discover what happens with death and much more. You need to consider the Astral not just in terms of going to another dimension, but what you can do there and what are the best things you can do there.

It is more exciting than anything you can read in a book or watch at the cinema; it is something that really happens to you. You actually find yourself in another dimension, existing outside the physical world. You will be able to fly, go through walls and objects, meet people and travel to distant places. It is a profound experience.

Will power is a key element in achieving it; you need to make the effort to push forward, because if you don't then you begin to slide down. You need to be persistent and continuous in your efforts.

This course will also teach you how to remember dreams and what you can do in the Astral if you enter it consciously. You can't really talk just about being in the Astral plane and not say what there is there and what the overall scheme of things is. That knowledge of the scheme of things is not a matter of religious belief but of experience, much of it gained in the Astral plane.

The spiritual is part of the Astral plane; you can't just explain about it without mentioning spiritual beings, because the Astral plane is their dwelling place. They live there just as we do here and if you travel enough you will meet them. The overall aim of the whole series of courses is not just to explain how to go into the Astral and meet spiritual beings, but how to become one. Going into the Astral plane is part of a spiritual search, it is used to get knowledge and information for the path of inner transformation. With the experience I have of all this, I can explain to you the process you need to go through.

DREAMS

Every night with sleep, dreams occur, whether they are remembered or not. In dreams the images from the subconscious become real, and one exists in the world that has been projected. However, not all dreams are projections of the subconscious; some actually take place in the Astral plane, while others are scenes or places that are put by ones own Being or by awakened beings (Masters).

This happens because with sleep, we leave behind the physical body, which holds the psyche within the physical plane, while sensory impressions enter the fifth dimension, what we call the Astral plane. We are connected to the physical body through a silver cord, which makes it impossible to not come back to the body after we have woken up. So while we dream, messages are sent from us, the psyche, in the Astral, to our physical body, including the brain and vice versa, through that silver cord.

Now being without a physical body, there is no physical world to see, touch and taste, so what is left are thoughts, emotions and consciousness, but you are in the Astral plane. Unfortunately, when there, what is actually in the Astral plane is not normally seen, or it is only seen partially because of the images of the mind, which are projected onto it. Even if what is seen there is real it is common not to even realise or question that you are there. It is the nature of that plane that one creates one's own world, which is not real. However, there is something real there, only it is not normally seen when dreaming. To see what is there, we must be aware (which we will explain more about in future classes) and be clear of the images projected by the subconscious.

When in the dreams, the process of daydreaming that occurred during the day continues. Dreams occur at night because of the daydream of thoughts, images and emotions of the subconscious (the egos) that take place during the day. Going through the day like that, one is rarely aware of the information of the five senses, of the reality of where one is at any given moment. Therefore, when sleep arrives, there is also a lack of awareness of where one is.

Sometimes when dreaming you do actually see what is there in the Astral. This is because there can sometimes be periods of lucidity. In these periods someone may see what really exists in the Astral world or dream about a place that actually exists in the physical world (even though they may never have seen it and discover it later physically). In these clear times higher beings can show you things or teach you and they can awaken the consciousness, clearing the projections of the subconscious in order to teach something. For example, you could have a premonition about something that will happen in the future, something which you could have had no way of knowing, yet you see the event in a dream and it comes true.

Sometimes the dreams themselves can have a symbolic meaning. The meaning of the scene or of the symbols shown in the dream can be intuitively comprehended, or if you have some knowledge of esoteric symbols, you can decipher the meaning of the dream as long as you apply intuition as well.

There is another type of dream that is the nightmare. These require more space and time to explain properly so I will leave it for another lesson in another course.

There is valuable information to be gained by studying dreams, both the meaningful ones and the ones created by the images and false scenarios projected by the subconscious. In this latter type, you may see yourself perhaps angry, fighting or stealing. They could be things that you would not usually do in everyday life, or they could be things that you usually do in everyday life. In either case, bizarre though they sometimes may be, they are an accurate reflection of what goes on in the psyche, in the conscious and subconscious processes during the day, during any day of one's life.

In the Self Knowledge course, you learn to see these different psychological states (egos) during daily life and learn how to study the dreams to get information about the states that occur during the day, for example, fear, anger or anxiety. On the Esoteric course, you learn how to get rid of the different elements of the subconscious and to replace them with consciousness. Gradually the subconscious decreases and one is more and more conscious at each moment during both dreams and in daily life.

The less time is spent in these subconscious states in daily life and the less we have them, the more the psyche increases in its consciousness and lucidity and as a consequence, the lucidity of the dreams increases, because they are directly related. In other words, the more aware we are in daily life, the more aware we are in dreams. Eventually then we will see the Astral exactly as it is, but that is really a part of a long process which I will explain more about as the different courses progress.

THE ASTRAL PLANE

The Astral is the first of two planes of the fifth dimension. There are seven dimensions in total. Most people know what the first three are and the fourth is known to science, which is time. Science in quantum physics postulates the likelihood of parallel universes existing and includes the fifth dimension in this, due to the discovery that minute particles behave unpredictably according to laws different to ours. They are correct in this, since the laws of the fifth dimension are different and it is at this molecular level that the physical and the fifth dimension meet.

Going to that dimension is, however, an internal science. To do it you have to explore the psyche and that is where science effectively leaves it. This is where we begin though, because this is an internal science; you study, experiment, experience and gain knowledge.

Being in the Astral is provable to those who do it, although there have been many cases of people seeing objects, places or events while out of the body, then later being able to tell others about them, while to observers they were asleep and had no way of knowing about them. It is something real; it is not a figment of the imagination, but another place that exists. We are all familiar in a way with the Astral, because it's the place that we go to in dreams. Except that in an Astral experience you are actually there and you can know that you are, in the same way that you know that you are in the physical world.

It is even possible to meet different people there, and that in fact was the first Astral experience I had. I was with a group doing a practice in a Gnostic Centre. The instructor had asked us to go into a room and to look at it, everything in it, very intensively. I remember observing everything in the room in great detail, then we went back into the other room. An object was placed in the room I had just observed and we had to go back there in the Astral and see what was put in it.

As I lay down, I concentrated on the room intensively, remembering all the little details that I had seen. Soon afterwards, I began to rise out of my body. I became very frightened and shouted "help, help!" but no one could hear me because I was in the Astral. I looked around and the instructor had projected, he was sitting there and another man had appeared in the room. Unfortunately, my fear brought me back to my body. I looked around and I was surprised that no one had heard me shouting.

Later on I spoke to the instructor and he confirmed that the gentleman whom we both knew had been there. Although it was brief, it was an amazing experience for me. I discovered that it is possible to leave the physical body and to meet with people there.

We only see a small part of life living here in the physical world, but through Astral travel, you see that there is much more. You then want to find out what it is all about, what exists there and why, so I will explain the whole picture as the course progresses.

If you try the Astral without knowing the whole picture you will not be able to do very much there of any real significance and will easily be confused, drawing misleading conclusions about it.

There are four ways to have an out-of-body experience. The first is to project, the second is to wake up in a dream, to know that you are in one and to realise that it is the Astral, the third is to have a near death experience and the fourth is with death.

I explain about the process of death on the Esoteric course, and teach techniques to achieve the first two. Not surprisingly, you can learn a lot about death from the Astral, because the dead go into the other dimensions, so you can see something of what happens.

The Astral is a whole new world to explore, but the main use that we have for it is for spiritual development. With it, you can see how you are doing; you can monitor your spiritual progress and can walk along the spiritual path knowing each step that you have made.

There you can see, meet and receive teachings from spiritual beings; those who have founded or have been mentioned in the world's great religions, in mythology, or in esotericism. You can travel to distant places in the world and beyond, you can get access to incredible knowledge that is denied to the majority of people in the world who do not go there consciously. However, you can get much more if you walk along the spiritual path, receiving knowledge and experience beyond what you can imagine.

The Astral itself, when it is not clouded by the projections of the mind, can look similar to the physical world. There you can see things that are here, as they are here. The things that are in the physical world are also in the Astral, so projecting into your bedroom at night, you can see it as it is in the physical. You can get up, walk out of your room and go outside. You can see the place, the town or city where you live, the outside of your house, the street, etc, all as they are in the physical.

Then, because it is the Astral and is governed by its own laws, you are able to fly. You can jump into the air and fly upwards, looking down over your house and the area where you live. It will look very often as it does normally. Then, as many people have done, you can fly somewhere.

Things do not always look the same though. Something may be different in your bedroom, you may project to a different place or strange things could be going on. It could be that the mind is projecting something, so you do not see it as it is, there are actually different things there, things have been placed there, or you have been put in a place for you to learn something.

You should pay close attention to what you see because it may be information for you, in the form of a symbol, a number, an event or words that are spoken. Information is often given there symbolically, so you need to use your intuition and to learn about the spiritual path and its symbolism, then you will decipher the correct meaning. You can learn to develop intuition on these courses.

Symbols are used because they are a universal language. Common symbols can be found throughout the great religions of the world.

In case you are wondering what kind of body you have in the Astral, I will explain more about it in the Esoteric course, because it requires too much explanation to fit here.

FEAR

Fear of the unknown is very common, but you learn to overcome the fear of being in the Astral through experience. For example, you may be afraid of eating a piece of fruit that you do not know anything about, however those who know about the fruit eat it and even enjoy it.

Fear is an ego and by understanding and eliminating egos, in this case fear (which you will learn about on our other courses), you gradually get rid of it.

Fear is also related to the overall state of the energies within the psyche. There is an practice called Alchemy that transforms the energies within the psyche. When the energies are weak there tends to be much more fear. Alchemy, which will be explained about in the Esoteric course, strengthens the energies.

THERE IS NO DANGER

Everyone Astral travels every night when dreaming. When you Astral project, you are aware of the whole process through which you (minus the physical body) go to the fifth dimension. When this process is new it can be very startling. Many people think that when they get into the Astral they are not going to come back, but people come back every night after dreaming. It is a normal part of life to leave the physical body behind for it to rest and recuperate its energies. We could not survive if we did not do that, it is just that with the process of Astral projection you are aware of the process that takes place when leaving the physical body and going into the Astral plane.

Another fear is that there can be entities there that will stop you from coming back or will harm you in some way. There are entities that exist in the Astral and we explain what they are and how to deal with them on this course, but they will not harm you physically in any case, so there is no need to worry about it.

WILL POWER FOR ASTRAL PROJECTION

Astral travel can take a lot of effort to maintain and achieve. To do it, you have to be determined and single-minded. You need to be clear in your goal to achieve it and to make whatever sacrifices are necessary.

It can sometimes take quite a long time to achieve, so patience, effort and determination are very important; they will lay the foundation for continuity. If it looks as though nothing is working don't give up, persist and you will eventually succeed.

~

WEEK I EXERCISES

The exercises on the course follow an order, which is designed to be effective for getting results. To get the Astral techniques to work you should do each one given every week in the order that they are given.

We begin with two simple ones. The first is a technique to relax the body and the second is one to remember your dreams when you wake up in the morning.

Exercise 1 - Relaxation

It is very important to learn to relax the body. The whole body needs to be relaxed for projection to take place. If you are tense it will be more difficult to focus upon the exercise you are doing and it will be more difficult for the Astral and physical bodies to separate and to fall asleep, as sleep is needed for Astral projection. This exercise of relaxation prepares you for the exercises that follow in this course.

This is a very simple technique and can be done easily; it is a matter of relaxing all the muscles in the body.

You need to lie down on your back with your legs straight and your arms by your side.

Go through each muscle relaxing them all one by one. You can start anywhere as long as you go through each muscle methodically, making each one completely relaxed.

Pay particular attention to the face once you get to it, there can be little areas of tension that are easily overlooked. Relax them all.

Once you have checked everywhere, repeat the procedure, just to make sure that there are no areas of tension that you have missed, or that have been reintroduced. The aim is to be totally relaxed.

In this state, you are now ready to begin your exercise of Astral projection.

Practice this every night before you go to sleep. When you go to do your exercise of projection you need to relax like this first, so for now do this exercise to get you ready for the techniques that will soon follow.

Exercise 2 - Remembering dreams

This is an exercise that you can do whenever you wake up from sleeping to remember your dreams. Dreams take place in the Astral plane and there is much to be learnt from them. Though much is projected by the mind, there can still be places that you have travelled to in the Astral plane within a dream and you can get much information from the scenes of dreams, the symbols in them and teachings that may have been given.

Remembering your dreams will give you an insight into your psychology and will get you used to the Astral realm you are going to explore. It is easy to miss many dreams that have occurred during sleep but here is a technique you can use to help remember them. Try it every morning, the more you do it the more you will develop your ability to recall them consistently. Bear in mind that as you go on in this course, you will learn to increase your level of awareness during daily life and so your dreams will become clearer and clearer.

When you wake up don't move.
Not even a finger, simply open your eyes and close them again and begin to remember your dreams from the first one you can remember. Try to see it in as much detail as you can, then you may find that more dreams appear. Carry on remembering the ones before if you can. It may take a bit of training not to move when you wake up, but if you try repeatedly, you begin to train your body. It is important not to move when you wake up because by moving, the physical and Astral bodies become merged and you become locked into the physical body, whereas when you just wake up, they often have a looser connection, which makes remembering dreams easier.

Pronounce the mantra Raom Gaom.
If you still cannot remember any dreams, continue to lie still for a little while with your eyes closed, to see if they appear. If they do not, then pronounce this mantra. A mantra is a series of sounds, a word, or words that have psychic effects. They have these effects depending upon the words or upon the sounds which are often based upon the vowels A, E, I, O, U. These vowels stimulate the chakras, which then increase certain psychic faculties. Each vowel corresponds to a certain chakra and increases a particular faculty.

In this case, the mantra for remembering dreams is called RAOM GAOM. You pronounce it elongating the sound of each letter like this: Rrraaaaaoooooommmmm Gaaaaaoooooommmmm.
    You can listen to the sound file at:
    http://www.gnosticweb.org/astralbook/Raom_Gaom.mp3

If you pronounce this mentally (not aloud), repeating it over and over again for a while, you will notice the dreams beginning to appear. As they do, concentrate upon each one. If you need to, pronounce it again several times and try to remember more and so on.

    If you want to, keep a diary or a record of your dreams. You may find that things you don't understand now you will do later, but make sure that no one else can see it or find it. This is because someone may find out things that are personal to you.

    To begin with, look into your dreams to see what sort of dreams you have, what different psychological elements such as anger or fear you can find and recognise. Look too, to see whether you have been to any places, whether you have been flying (because we can fly in that plane), whether there are any symbols (a form of communication in the Astral plane) that you can recognise and intuitively capture the meaning of, whether you had any teachings, or even had mystical experiences.

If you are in doubt about what you see and don't understand it, try using your intuition to work it out.

~

QUESTIONS AND ANSWERS

Below are some questions that I have answered on the Astral generally and on remembering dreams:

Astral Travel

Q. Is there ever any chance I will not be able to get back to my physical body after I have been Astral travelling?

A. We go to the Astral every night when we go to sleep. The only difference with Astral travelling is that we are aware of the fact that we are in another dimension. In fact, you usually get pulled back to your body too soon. The hard part is staying out there.

Is Astral travel the same as lucid dreaming?

Astral travel includes lucid dreaming and also travel after a conscious projection. It is being self-aware in the Astral plane of the fifth dimension.

Is it possible to attract the attention of people in the "physical" world and interact with them while I move about in my Astral travels?

You are extremely unlikely to be able to interact with people who are in the physical while you are in the Astral. The person in the physical needs to have polyvision active to be able to do that.

Can I move objects in the Astral environment?

You can move Astral objects in the Astral environment, just as you can move physical ones in the physical environment.

Can I move forward or back through time to any period that I wish? If this is so, can I go back in time and change events, like preventing myself from making a bad decision?

You can move backwards in time in the Astral, but not truly forwards. Although you can see events that are going to happen while in the Astral, it is often not 100% certain that all of them will happen because it is possible to change circumstances here in the physical world and that alters what will eventually materialise. Usually though, things do not change here and what is seen there materialises here. You cannot go back in time to change events because what you see of the past are the Akashic Records. You step into what are basically records of what has happened. You cannot change events.

Is it true that only certain people can Astral travel, and that it is the kind of thing you inherit "genetically"?

No. Anyone can learn to Astral travel, I had never done it until I was taught how.

How do I ask for help from my guides when I am trying to project?

Presuming that you mean beings that have awakened for light, you call the name of the being. For example, if you call the Master Anubis, you call "Master Anubis, I invoke you" or words to that effect, repeatedly. If you ever advance far enough on the esoteric path, you can choose a being that can help you personally.

I was wondering if taking Prozac or any other antidepressants some how affect your brain making you unable to Astral project?

Yes they will affect your Astral, making it more difficult. They affect the consciousness, which needs to be as clear as possible.

Can drugs (alcohol, marijuana, psychedelics) help you get out of your body?

They can damage your Astral body, make the mind and emotions more active and can make your consciousness more asleep, all of which are not good for continuing Astral success, not to mention the spiritual work. Cultures like the Shamans use them for projections, but they can only go to the inferior Astral and get experiences that look spiritual sometimes, but which in fact belong to the negative side. I have seen their ceremonies in the Astral so I know about that. All drug-induced experiences belong to the negative side and that side is only strengthened in a person by taking drugs.

I just wondered if it was possible to meet with other human beings whilst Astral travelling. Either while they are Astral travelling too or while they are awake and their friend comes to see them by Astral travel.

Yes you can meet with other human beings whilst Astral travelling, but to talk to them meaningfully, they also have to be conscious in the Astral. Otherwise, if we find them and they are dreaming they will look like drunken people. They are unlikely to recognise us although they may remember seeing us in a dream. You can see people who are awake in the physical because you see their Astral part, but you cannot communicate with them because they will not be able to see you (unless they have polyvision).

How do I get my eyes open when I am in the Astral?

It is quite common to see darkness or to be unable to open your eyes at the beginning, as you are not used to the Astral or your Astral body. Sometimes the Astral can be dark even if our eyes are open. There are techniques called conjurations that you can use which help to get rid of negative influences that can often cause this.

Can reduced eating daily help out-of-body experiences?

Some people say that they find OBE's easier when they eat lightly, however the main problem people have with Astral projection is that there is a lack of concentration. All you need for Astral projection is concentration and sleep, so how much you eat should not have much of an effect. Having said that, it is not so good to try an Astral exercise or to go to bed after a very heavy meal because if it upsets the stomach it can take you into lower parts of the Astral. You need to be careful about eating less, fasting and so on, because it can cause other problems. As long as you are eating sensibly, I suggest you keep your regular eating pattern and continue practising in order to improve your concentration and OBE experiences.

I really want to learn how to do this but I am scared that when I do start to split, I will become frightened and will not get to enjoy the experience.

That fear is only natural to start with, but you will overcome it as you practice. Even if you do become afraid when you split the first time, in retrospect you will cherish the experience because it is something so new and magical, and it will confirm the reality of it for you. Then after that you will be able to approach it with more stability, and it will become better and more magical if you persist.

Are there any moral implications to mystically uniting with a soul in the Astral plane who is married in the physical plane?

Yes, we would not advise that be done; the Esoteric course explains more about why that is.

Every time I try to Astral project I lie there for a long time and I feel things but I never seem to make it.

If you are feeling all sorts of Astral sensations, try to get up out of bed like you would in the morning. It is not always true that we project into the air when we split. We sometimes split but remain on our bed, feeling like we still have not split. So then, you need to carefully get out of bed and take a little jump to float - and you may get a pleasant surprise.

I am very interested in gaining spiritual knowledge through

Astral travel but is it also possible to gain knowledge on any other subjects while out travelling -information we can use in the physical?

The Astral plane is full of all sorts of knowledge about our inner psychology, about the past, present and future. You could learn about ancient cultures, nature, divinity, the process of life and death. You could see if there is life on other planets and much more. It is a completely new dimension to discover. The learning is endless. It can also reveal earthly things.

If I Astral travel, is my body sleeping and resting so that I wake up refreshed as always, or will it be tired after travelling? And after starting to travel, will I be able to return to normal sleep?

Yes, if we Astral travel, the body sleeps just the same as normal, so when we wake up, we feel refreshed the same as normal too. Once you start to Astral travel, you need to keep doing the exercises to keep going there, otherwise very little usually happens and the sleep goes back to normal. At the end of travelling, you usually go back to your body and wake straight up in it, or the Astral turns into a dream and you wake up the next morning usually remembering that you have travelled.

What is the difference between an out of body experience and Astral projection?

Out-of-body experiences cover all experiences in the Astral, while Astral projection refers specifically to projecting out of your physical body into the fifth dimension.

When you project, why can you still see things on the material plane?

When you project, you are not seeing actual physical matter but the Astral part of what is in the physical world, because everything that exists here also exists there.

I get to the point which I believe is right before separation but I still see only blackness. Then I start worrying about my eyelids and wonder if I am supposed to somehow see through them upon projection.

This is a common problem. You will not normally see through your eyelids, you need to open them. Sometimes when trying to split we can suddenly seem to "see through our eyelids", but we are then already in our Astral body with our eyes open. Try not to confuse the functions of the two bodies: the physical body and the Astral body. Once you feel you have separated, I would suggest firstly getting up out of bed carefully, as you would in the morning, perhaps just sitting on the bed. Then open your eyes just as naturally.

My friend has seen me watching her almost every night but I am not aware of it at the time she sees me. It is when I am in a deep sleep and usually on the hour after midnight. Can you tell me why I am not aware?

There could be two reasons: your friend could be seeing your Astral body while your physical body is asleep. While we are asleep, we go to different places during the night. It is possible that you unconsciously end up at your friend's place. Alternatively, while your friend is asleep she thinks of you and a projection of her thought (which is an image of you) appears in the Astral looking at her. This is because in the Astral all our thoughts turn into real scenarios of life, which we call dreams, some more than others.

While trying a practice of Astral projection, I saw dark shapes (shadowy, dark clouds) moving around the room. In fear I snapped out of the practice feeling very scared.

Fear is something that can be overcome. The negative things you perceived could have come from your subconscious, although they are more likely to be negative entities in the Astral. To deal with them you will need to know about conjurations, which we use to expel negative entities of any kind.

Is there any chance that someone else could get into my physical body while I am off travelling in my Astral body?

No. There is no danger of that happening. You are attached to your own physical body by the silver chord, so only you can get in, that is unless you decide to become a medium or to channel, in which case all kinds of negative entities can get in without you knowing (not recommended).

What is the best way to get rid of an unwanted attacker while trying to leave the body?

To deal with them properly you need to use the conjurations, which are explained on the course.

Can other beings within the Astral plane sever the silver cord?

The cord is severed by divine beings when the appointed moment of death arrives.

What is the difference between lucid dreaming and Astral projection?

The difference between lucid dreaming and Astral projection is that you project from your body while sleep arrives, while in lucid dreaming you wake up in the Astral from a dream. Sometimes though in lucid dreaming, the dream images can distort what is there. As long as you are not affected by those, you can be in the same place, do the same things, etc.

OK, this question might sound a little bit weird. I don't know if its got anything to do with Astral projection or not, but before I Astral projected for the first time a few months ago, I heard singing. It was a woman singing, although I could not make out what she was singing. It was as if it was far away in the distance, and it was definitely not outside my head (this sounds weird) but I had to listen inwards to hear it. Do you know what this means?

You can hear sounds from the other dimensions. This is called clairaudience. You usually hear them in the transition period between wakefulness and sleep. It indicates that you were probably assisted in your projection.

Voices of a different kind can also be heard in that transition period before going into the Astral or to sleep. These come from the egos when they are leaving the physical body to go into the fifth dimension. They sound like shouts, moans and babble. These were not the ones you heard at that time, but it is worth knowing about if it happens to you in the future.

My friend who is interested in Astral travel told me that while out of the body, if there is a spirit around your body while your spirit is away travelling, it can take over your body. Is that true?

No, a spirit cannot take over your body like that.

Hi, I was just beginning to do the exercises and looking forward to Astral travelling (hopefully). I am curious whether I can go to a place that I want to go to in the real world when I Astral travel. Say if I want to go to an exact place at an exact time, is it possible?

You can travel to any place in the physical world but you will see its Astral part, not the physical one, because you are in a different dimension and you see the things that are there. The dimensions intermingle and everything that is in the physical has an Astral part.

Hi, I have read and heard many rumours about things you can do while Astral travelling e.g. go back and forwards in time. So I was wondering would you be able to come into contact with departed relatives or loved ones through Astral travel? I would be grateful for any information on this subject.

You can go back in time, because it has already happened and everything is recorded in Akashic files. The future is different. Events permeate down the different dimensions until they reach here. So we can see, or be in things that are yet to happen. However, sometimes our actions here can change the events that were going to happen.

You can come into contact with departed relatives or loved ones through Astral travel, because a recently deceased person is in the other dimensions. You mostly see their personality which is what we probably recognise as the person. You can talk to them and they recognise you.

If the "Astral plane" as you refer to it is only our "dream state", is the "Astral body" then not real? What I mean is this: say, I become adept at Astral travel. As my family lives far away, say for example I get the feeling that my sister is unhappy or in trouble, and I want to check on her. Can I travel in my Astral body to where

she is located, in her physical body, unaware of me, and check that she is all right? In other words, can the Astral body travel through the physical world and, although it is obviously removed from the physical, still view the physical plane as it exists in physical reality? Or is everything you would experience in the Astral body necessarily "false". That is, if I told myself I wanted to go to see my sister and suddenly I was there next to her, asleep or whatever, is that my real sister in her real bedroom at home in the real world or is it just a dream "vision" of my sister?

Just wondering because sometimes I worry about her so much and would like to check on her in this way, but if it is "false" and just a dream, then what is the point?

The Astral plane is real, but we often don't see it accurately when we are in the dream state, because of the projections of the subconscious. However, when we Astral travel, we are no longer dreaming and can see what is really there.

So yes you can travel in your Astral body to see the real her. You will see the Astral counterpart of her physical body and she will be unaware of you unless she is travelling too, but she may remember seeing you in her dreams if she is dreaming herself.

Everything that exists in the physical world also exists in the Astral, so if you throw a shoe on the roof of your house in the physical for example, you can go and see where it landed in the Astral, then you can find it where you saw it if you check later in the physical.

That is great, thanks Mark. Now another question that kind of follows on from this one: say I go to visit my sister and she wakes up while I am there. Will she see me? Is the Astral body visible to those not in the Astral plane? Or will she maybe "feel" my presence on some other, non-visual, intuitive level? If I speak to her, will she hear me, or will my voice enter her mind as thoughts?

It is unlikely that she will see, hear or feel you. Things are taking place in the Astral all the time and they are normally not perceived.

That has not to say however that it cannot happen, because there are many latent psychic faculties that would allow it to happen. These are increased with the esoteric works that we are carrying out on this course, but normally she would not perceive anything.

I just wanted to know if there are any rules that we should follow when in the Astral. I do not want to get there and do something that will offend anyone or anything! Also if you went to the Astral and saw something like a building that only existed in the Astral, and you described it to me and then I went to look at it, would I see the same thing as you or is the building represented to us based on our own individual experiences and thoughts (if that is how things work at all in the Astral)?

You need to know much more about what is happening in general to know what not to do and what is best to do.

However, you can still use your commonsense and intuition, remembering that you are there primarily to receive spiritual information. Of course don't do anything sexual or go along with any evil entities, or do anything that you know to be wrong.

Things can sometimes be there because they do exist in the Astral and others can see them; there are many things that exist there that do not exist here. However, things can also be put there as a teaching for us, or they could be projections of the mind. Again you can use your intuition and gain experience, because experience makes things gradually clearer.

Remembering Dreams

I find if I come out of a dream that I do not want to leave I just remain still. If I just had a nightmare and don't want to fall asleep into it again I change body positions.

You are likely to move as soon as you wake up from a nightmare because of the fright. Nightmares are different from normal dreams, they occur in a different place. We will explain more about these in detail as the course goes on.

It is possible to avoid recurring nightmares and also to avoid nightmares altogether. I used to have them, but I do not any more thanks to this work. As you progress in these studies, you will learn more about the Astral and about psychology and you will eventually be able to prevent them altogether.

Just a little tip for now to avoid the likelihood of having nightmares: avoid having a large meal before you go to sleep.

In addition, taking drugs that alter consciousness increases the chance of nightmares, so for this and many other reasons it is better to avoid them. I will also be explaining about drugs on the Self Knowledge course.

I have read the introductory lesson and I have these following questions relating to the general topic: Usually when I wake up, I cannot remember my dreams at all. Is there anything else I could try other than the mantra? Next thing I would like to know about is, whenever I have a nightmare I always prove to myself in the dream that "it is only a dream and there is nothing to worry about." At that point the dream either ends or I gain control of it for a while and it ends soon after. What does this mean? The last thing is that the reason I cannot remember some of my dreams is because they are always so abstract and unstable. The scenery is always warped and constantly changing, so are all the people, as well as my emotions. Nothing ever stays the same for more than a couple of seconds and nothing seems logical or orderly. Please, I hope you can explain this. Thank You.

Bear in mind that the technique for remembering dreams needs to be practiced. The memory is trained with it and so it improves with practice.

In the dreams where you had control, you were partially awake psychically there. So if you are in a dream and you know that it is a dream, say to yourself that you are in the Astral and jump with the intention of flying. You will see that you can fly and can then travel to different places. If it is a nightmare though, or has unpleasant things in it, you need to use some techniques called conjurations that we will explain soon on the course.

You have to take what happens in dreams, and the ability to remember them, as part of an overall psychological study. The reason why they are so abstract and unstable is because of the state of the psyche itself, as they reflect it.

With the psychological work, you will be able to create more order within and to have dreams that are more coherent. They are also related to the level of awareness we have in daily life, the more aware, the clearer the dreams.

I tend to remember my dreams and I have been trying to write them down, which I am bad about doing. There was one I remember

WEEK I AN INTRODUCTION TO DREAMS AND ASTRAL TRAVEL - 23

in particular where I was flying around a very high mountain. I feel pretty sure it was in Tibet or that area. I remember becoming lucid and trying to change the direction of my flight. I could not control it and then I lost the dream. Is this common? Is there something I could have done that might have helped me control this experience better or was I just not ready?

Yes, it is very common to lose the Astral like that, particularly if you are not experienced at it. The more you do it the more you learn how to stay there and to go where you want. Treat it as a learning experience and try to see what happened at the point that you lost it.

Having more awareness while you are there and learning to concentrate when you want to go somewhere will also help, as will the work on transmutation, which is in a later topic.

I am aware that flying dreams are usually Astral travel. My most recent one was of flying throughout a gigantic Antique Store. Most of my dreams that have really left an impression on me have been dreams that deal with antiques. Do the "antiques" have any real significance?

Very much depends on the context of the dream. Intuition (that is catching the first feeling you had about the dream when you woke up) can usually give you the right direction.

Antiques can be projections of your subconscious, or they can be more symbolic. For example, they could symbolise something ancient that you have to uncover with the spiritual work, or they could relate to the state of your spiritual work at the moment.

I was aware that I was in bed, but I was also sitting at the foot of the bed, and a being swathed in black and a very deep black came into the room. At first I was rather interested, then fear took over. As it approached me, I started to fight it. I remember while doing this I could not move my real body. I continued to fight and try to speak but I was paralysed. I finally woke up. This scared me quite a bit. Has anyone else had an experience like this?

Experiences like this are quite common and are well recorded in history. You were paralysed because you were in the transition period between being awake and asleep, and so did not have movement of the

physical body.
> What you perceived coming towards you was a sinister entity. There is nothing to be frightened about though, they can be there at any time, it is just that you were aware of its presence then. Later in the course you will have a technique that you can use to get rid of anything like that.

After reading the exercise, I am not sure how I will be able to do this. I usually wake up with an alarm clock. When it goes off, my first reaction is to slap the snooze button. So once I am awake, I have already moved. In between snooze button slaps I can usually fall back asleep.
What would you recommend I do? I am not sure if I can give up the alarm clock - I would never get to work on time!

It is possible to train yourself to wake up before the alarm goes off, but you will still need to have the alarm anyway, it is just one of those things of modern life.

If you can wake up before the alarm goes off, it is much better and you don't need the snooze button, just the first alarm.

If the alarm wakes you up, you just have to try the mantra or concentrate, so that the dreams can be remembered before the snooze button goes off. The concentration and dream recall can improve the more you practice it.

I have a question about a dream I had [dream edited out...]

I cannot go into details of people's dreams because they are so personal to the dreamer. It is best not to say much or anything about dreams or Astral experiences that have an esoteric side because darkness follows and we don't see things for a while. Esoteric knowledge is secret.

I awoke one morning early enough to practice the mantra. It seemed to work and I was remembering dreams, that is until I heard a voice so crystal clear and it seemed to be right beside my head in bed. It startled me so much that I jumped away from it almost in a fighting stance to protect myself. My question: are voices such as this evidence of the Astral?

Yes, because you have been practicing you are more receptive to the Astral and because you still had a slight connection there, as the Astral body had not quite merged with the physical one. Sometimes higher beings can speak and you can hear them like that. This is different to the voices of the egos, which sound like yells, screams, etc.

I just started this course and dreaming is not a problem here. I dream every night and most of the time I remember them. My dreams are crazy ones though. I dream of seeing new homes for my family members, seeing unknown objects in the night sky and more than once seeing different shapes of stars that move like foreign objects up there, just moving across the dark night sky. I have had that one more than I care to mention. I mostly dream of family and material things we get here on earth. Do you have an answer for these?

It is best for you to find the answers to your own dreams because they relate to you, but you need to learn how. It will help if you know more about esoteric symbolism and use your intuition.

You can learn to develop intuition. This will help you to differentiate between a projection from your subconscious and something that has meaning. It will also help you to capture that meaning. If you see strange things in your dreams, you can use them to wake up in the Astral. Sometimes they are placed in dreams for that purpose.

Can you advise how we are supposed to use the Raom Gaom mantra? Is it something we should repeat as we fall asleep, or first thing in the morning when we awake? Thanks!

It is something you should do when you wake up. Lie still and close your eyes, repeating the mantra in your mind until the dream images appear.

Maybe it is beginner's luck. Last night, I had two lucid dreams, including a flying dream. In the first, I was aware I was dreaming and able to direct it. I was able to focus sharply on things and even read small text, which did not make much sense. In the second, I was able to fly where I wanted, for a while at least.

My question is what does this mean? It was a nice experience,

and I will try to duplicate it, but what context is there for this and what is the next step? Also, doing the first exercise of remembering the dream before completely waking up has helped me to retain a good bit of it, though a lot has faded.

You are being helped by spiritual beings to learn about the Astral. If you or anyone makes real efforts to try these exercises, you can get a good deal of help.

The next step is to continue with what you are doing and to try the exercises that are going to be given with much patience.

I have been practicing the Raom Gaom mantra for four days, and always yield the same result... I fall asleep again and have another dream.
The interesting part is that I can recall this subsequent dream easily, as if it was a real life memory from the previous day. The dreams are mostly a lecture-like session about dreams, fears and feelings. In one of the dreams, someone gave me a book about interpreting dreams and he taught me how to read the index and find threads.
From this book, I re-discovered a description of my inner fear that has been forgotten for a long time. Is this normal or should I remain awake? I am afraid that these subsequent dreams were only dreams and that I have not actually learned anything.

Even though you are falling asleep you are being taught and are benefiting from it. Keep going with what you are doing.

Can you tell me if it is possible to control our dreams? Sometimes I am aware of my dreams, so when I know that I am dreaming, I can do almost anything in my dream. For example, by thinking of objects to appear in my hands, they appear just as I had visualised in my mind. So can you tell me if it is possible, because I doubted it?

Yes, you can do that. What you think of can materialise, but it is not a good idea because then you will not see what is actually there. It is best to be aware, because then you can get real information and teachings, rather than seeing what is in your mind.

Week 2

How to Astral Project

ASTRAL PROJECTION

Astral projection is the act of consciously leaving the physical body and going into the Astral plane of the fifth dimension. Every time we go to sleep, this takes place unconsciously, but there are techniques to go there consciously. On this course, I will explain some that I have seen to be most effective.

Sleep is required to project, because it is with sleep that the Astral body separates from the physical one. The two bodies are attached by a silver cord, which stretches infinitely. It sends messages between one body and the other, which enables the person in the Astral body to go back to the physical body as soon as they wake up from sleep.

When you carry out the Astral projection technique, it causes you to go through the process of sleep consciously. You are then aware of all the processes (sometimes just some of them) that take place within the transition period between wakefulness and sleep, until the two bodies separate.

In this topic, we will look at techniques to prepare for the Astral and one very effective technique of Astral projection.

ESTABLISHING THE FOUNDATION FOR ASTRAL TRAVEL - FOCUSING THE MIND AND BEING AWARE

Before we look into a technique for Astral projection, it is important to prepare the grounds for it. If you can get the first two exercises in this topic right it will be easier to get into the Astral, and you will be able to go into the Astral much more often. If you do not do this, the techniques given to project are less likely to work.

To successfully project, you need to concentrate on the exercise you are doing, without being distracted by other thoughts or by anything else. To be able to do this there are two basic exercises that help to prepare for it:

1. To be aware of whatever activity you are doing in a given moment in daily life.
2. To practice concentration/visualisation each day.

When you are aware of whatever activity you are doing in a given moment in daily life, you train the mind to be focused upon one thing and cut down the chatter. Therefore, when you do your exercise of projection you are more able to concentrate upon the exercise.

You also prepare for the techniques of Astral projection by learning to visualise, because many of the techniques use visualisation. To develop the ability to do this, you carry out exercises of visualisation. These train you to visualise and train the mind to concentrate on one thing intensively. Then, when you go to project, the mind is already trained to concentrate and visualise and the projection is more likely to succeed.

In both trying to Astral project and to be aware of what you are doing in daily life, the main obstacle is the continuous chattering and daydreaming of the mind.

THE PROBLEM OF THE CHATTERING MIND

Much of the failure in Astral projection comes because the mind is not trained to be on one thing. It is used to chattering away all day, then when you try to do an exercise to project, the mind carries on chattering. The thoughts that were so active during the day continue to be active and they interrupt the technique that you are doing, therefore Astral projection fails. Therefore, we are going to look into training it, thereby increasing the ability to focus it on whatever we need to.

It is of course necessary to use the mind in order to think and plan, remember things, solve problems, create/invent things, carry out tasks etc. However, the problem is that its activity is so compulsive; it just runs of its own accord. It is difficult for it to be on one thing and to be profoundly concentrated for any period of time. Rather it is scattered and the thoughts go on and on, like a wheel turning around and around. It should be a tool that is used. Indeed, it becomes one if we progress enough on the esoteric path, but in any case the mind must be focused in order to experience the Astral and that takes training. It is not something that happens overnight, it requires a great deal of effort but it is something that we can start with right away at this stage of the course and which will benefit everything that follows.

If you are not concentrated when trying to project then you will either be taken into sleep by a thought, or you will become restless and unable to sleep. Either way, being able to concentrate fixes the problem.

By having the mind chattering all day, it causes one to live in a state of daydreaming during daily life rather than being aware of each moment. This daydreaming continues at night except that it becomes real in the Astral plane and produces the dreams. By learning to be focused on what you are doing during the day, by being aware of what you are doing at any given moment, you are learning to act with consciousness, rather than simply thinking all the time. If you do this throughout the day, the mind will be less active at night when you want to project and you will have greater awareness in your dreams. Ultimately, if you can learn to be in consciousness and to use the mind as a tool, it is possible to direct the mind at will to any task such as projection, and to be successful at it.

The ability to have control over the mind and to use it effectively as a tool is ultimately part of a much deeper esoteric work. The different elements that make up the mind and emotions, which we call "egos", have to be observed and eliminated. A new kind of Astral and Mental body needs to be built and the consciousness radically transformed. These are beyond the scope of this Astral course and will be explained in the Esoteric course.

~

WEEK 2 EXERCISES

For now we will look into two very simple but very effective ways to prepare for the Astral; to be aware of what you are doing in daily life and to train the mind to concentrate and visualise.

Exercise 1

Being aware of what you are doing during the day

If you can get used to being focused upon what you are doing then, when you go to Astral project, you are used to being on one thing and the mind has much less activity. When we are on one thing, the mind gets quietened.

This also has an effect upon the quality and type of dreams at night. At night, all kinds of dreams take place; many of these (although not all) are projections from the subconscious. What happens during the day in the psyche continues at night in dreams, it is just that there is no physical body to bring you back to the world when dreaming. Therefore, the various images of the mind are projected onto the Astral plane and those things become real in the dreams. By waking up and being more aware, more conscious of what you are doing during the day, the same thing happens at night, you are more aware and more conscious of what you are doing. In another topic, I will give the technique whereby you can realise that you are in a dream and explore the Astral in that way.

The important thing is to concentrate upon whatever activity you are doing at the time and to do only one activity at a time. Even if you have many tasks to do and are under pressure, deal with the most important one, giving it your full attention, even if it is just for a few moments before you have to do another task. Give whatever you are doing at that moment your full attention.

You need to be aware of whatever you are doing throughout the day. This can be difficult to do, but to help you to get to that, concentrate upon three activities that you do each day, making the effort to use them to practice being aware of what you are doing. Any activity can be used, but try the following three. However well or difficult other things are going during the day, use these three activties to anchor yourself in awareness:

1. Washing yourself.
2. Putting your shoes on and taking them off.
3. Eating.

Concentrate upon each of these activities, not allowing the mind to interfere. If you have thoughts, go straight back to the activity you are doing, investigate how concentration works, then apply it throughout the day.

Exercise 2

Concentration/Visualisation

Moving onto the second technique to help prepare to Astral project, practice concentration/visualisation for ten minutes each day.

Take an object; it can be any object (one popular object for this exercise is a lit candle). Sit down and place it where you can see it clearly. Then, concentrate upon it in great detail, observing how it looks, it is texture, shape, colour, the material it is made of, the way that light reflects on it, etc, discovering everything you can about it. When you have clearly seen it, then close your eyes and recreate the object exactly as it is in your mind. If there are things that you cannot recreate because you did not look at them properly, or if the image is fading away, open your eyes and look at it again, study it, then close your eyes and recreate the image again in your mind. Keep doing this process so that you visualise it as clearly as you can.

This type of exercise gently trains the mind in visualisation and concentration, which are vital for Astral projection. Try to do it regularly, at least once a day for ten minutes at a different time from your Astral projection exercise; whenever is convenient for you.

If you want to do this for more times each day then do it, but increase it very gradually, because the mind needs to be educated and you should not force it.

HOW TO ASTRAL PROJECT

There are two main techniques used for Astral projection: concentration/ visualisation and mantras. I will explain more about mantras in another topic and will give the different visualisation techniques as the course progresses.

To begin to Astral project, I will give an effective technique you can try which is concentration/visualisation on the heart.

Sleep is needed to be able to project because it is with sleep that we detach from the physical body. Therefore, you need to be in a position in which you can sleep, lying down in bed for example. The best position for lying down is on your back, so I recommend that you do that. Then you need to be able to relax the body (as explained in last week's topic) because tension holds us into it. Without moving, go straight from the relaxation to practising Astral projection.

Exercise 3

A Technique for Astral Projection: Concentration on the Heart
For this Astral exercise, you can try concentrating on the heart. I have found this to be a very good technique to use. It is one of the main techniques for Astral projection.

The heart is not only a vital organ of the physical body, but in esotericism, it also has a spiritual aspect.

There are different ways of concentrating on the heart, but begin with this one first and if you wish, experiment with the other ways over the next two weeks. I will mention the other ways after explaining the first exercise to begin with:

The Exercise
After lying down on your back and relaxing, concentrate on the heart. Try to be aware of the heart beating. Feel each beat and concentrate upon each one of them. If you cannot feel it you can imagine it beating, but the more you learn the exercise, the easier it is to feel the heart beating without any aid.

If you really focus your mind on it, you can begin to project. There are a number of different things, sensations, etc, which happen as we leave the body. You may feel all of them, some of them, or none of them, in which case you may just find yourself there in the Astral without being aware of projecting.

After relaxing, you may feel that your body becomes very heavy, yet at the same time, strangely you feel very light. As you concentrate on the heart you may find the beats intensifying, hear a small noise, a very high-pitched whirring, like a motor inside your head, and a feeling of not being able to move. Then, a kind of an electric sensation may pass through the body. As this happens, you may feel yourself rising up, lifting up out of the body. As you lift, you have projected. You are in the Astral.

Sometimes during the exercise, you may get a feeling of immobilisation, but do not worry, let the projection happen. Continue with the exercise and you can eventually float upwards. Do not be distracted by any of the sensations that are taking place or you can lose it. If you are sure that you have projected but feel as though you cannot move, as though you are paralysed, then roll over on your side and get up that way.

You may have projected just a little way, in which case you may wonder whether you are actually out of the body, so you can check to verify that you have actually projected. To do this, get up from the bed, do it really, not mentally but do it very slowly and deliberately, without sharp, sudden movements. Then you will see that you are in the Astral. Look around at the place you are in, whether the room is exactly like it is normally, if there is anything strange.

If you are still not sure, then jump in the air and try to fly. If it is the Astral, you can fly and a completely new dimension is open to you to explore. Just do not try jumping out of the window.

If you have projected higher, then you know that you are in the Astral. You can explore by walking outside your house and flying, or by concentrating on or visualising a place that you want to go to, and then you go there rapidly.

The sensations of projecting can sometimes be different to the way that I have just described. For example, when you are concentrating you may feel the beats intensifying. As they get stronger, you feel that you are moving with them and the sensation increases as you go higher and higher with each beat, until you rise up out of the body.

As I explained earlier, I found my first experience a bit frightening, going into the unknown, not knowing if I would ever come back. However, experience has taught me not to worry. We dream every night, we are in the Astral but nothing bad ever happens to us. We are not stuck out there; we have a silver cord that attaches our Astral body to the physical body. It stretches infinitely long and is never broken unless we die, which does not happen by projecting and it does not just snap (although there is a limit to how far we can go in the universe). Nor can we get out and not be able to find a way back. The silver cord always pulls us back. We only have to move during sleep or wake up and we are back in the body. The difficulty is staying out there long enough. It is so easy to get pulled back. You usually begin to fade away, or travel backwards at a rapid pace until you fall back into the body.

There are sometimes negative entities in the Astral. I will explain about these soon in another topic and show you how to deal with them - do not worry, you will survive until then.

It can help to hold onto an object so that you are not pulled back so quickly while you are there. It is also important to watch that there are no large emotions or egos such as fear, or elation at being there, because these can be enough to pull us back straightaway. You also need to be as aware as possible and to maintain that awareness for as long as you can. Any daydreams there actually turn into dreams and before you know it, you are in a dream and you do not realise that you projected until you wake up from sleep.

The Astral is best done in a relaxed way; forcing it can interfere with the exercise, so it is important not to force it. Do it for as long as your body allows. It is better to gradually train the body, and then you become trained to sleep like this instead of falling asleep in the usual way. Sometimes you may be trying and not be able to sleep, so when you feel that you have tried for long enough, change to a more comfortable position that is better for sleep.

It is important to practise this exercise a lot, because it can be difficult. The more you try the more you learn about it. Much persistence, patience and dedication is required. You need to keep going every night, even if you have no success for a while, then all of a sudden you find that it works. If you do not keep going then what you have built up can quickly be lost and you have to build up the daily momentum again.

Ways to Concentrate on the Heart
There are different ways of concentrating on the heart. Here are some of them. Explore them over the next two weeks and find out which works best for you:

1. Feeling the heart beats
You simply direct your attention to your heart with the purpose of focusing on your heartbeats, trying to feel them throughout the body until your whole body is a heartbeat. If you maintain the concentration on the heart beat without random thinking, you should be able to Astral project.

2. Visualising the physical heart

Direct your attention to the heart with the purpose of focusing on your physical heart inside yourself through visualisation. That is, explore the heart in detail everywhere; the chambers, the arteries attached to the heart, the texture of the muscle, surfaces, etc. Explore in this way the inner and outer parts of the heart, try to find out how and why it is made that way, using your imagination, which gives you an instant insight into it if you do it right.

3. Visualising your heart as a temple

Direct your attention to your heart and visualise it being like a temple, a place with light and with the layout of a temple as you imagine or know one to be.

4. Feeling the heart beats throughout the body

Concentrate your attention on the tip of your nose until you feel the pulse in it. Afterwards, go to the right ear until you feel the pulse of the heart in it, then you continue with the left ear and the nose again feeling fully the pulse of the heart separately in each part where you have fixed your attention.

You can vary this with different parts of the body, be it in the tip of the nose or in the ear, in the arm, the foot, etc., and also throughout the whole body.

You can also try to slow down the pulse with concentration, which in turn can slow the heart beat and lead to an Astral split.

Gradually get used to any of these techniques, particularly lying down on your back if you are not used to it. Start with 10 minutes and then if you feel tired just go to sleep and try again the next time you wake up in the night or early in the morning. It could work at any time. For example if you wake up just 30 minutes before getting up from bed, that could be the time that it works.

Do not be afraid of not being able to go to sleep because this will only be an obstacle for your exercise. It will not let you try the exercise whole-heartedly and your efforts will be wasted.

If you feel that you can carry on with the exercise for more than 10 minutes do so, but do not force yourself. Forcing is counter-productive because then you do not feel like doing it the next day as you have experienced discomfort.

If you try to project more often, it is much better as the body and the mind get used to it without being forced. You enjoy the exercise and you want to do more of it. This is very important, because for Astral projection you need consistency, which means you need to try literally every night because that is how you learn how to do the exercise and you can correct whatever you are doing wrong.

There is a need not only to make efforts, but also to make those efforts properly. If you do not do an exercise just because you do not feel like it, you will be giving in to laziness and will be far less successful.

If you try it sporadically, then you are just fighting the odds, you are always a beginner and you never go further into the exercise itself, but only hope for a lucky chance. On the other hand, you should not force your body and mind when doing an exercise to the point of agony just because you want a result quickly. As you can see, there is a need for a methodical approach to the exercise.

Another very useful approach to improve at Astral projection when using the technique of concentration on the heart is to try the exercise for 10 minutes well before going to sleep. This is because you become more familiar with the exercise. You then have less chances of being taken away with thoughts and you know exactly what you need to do for that particular exercise that night.

Astral projection can be a very sensitive exercise. If you do anything out of place, the exercise can be over in a split second. By that, I mean that during the exercise, feelings of fear or excitement, or getting involved with the process that is taking place, wanting to almost make it happen by trying to accelerate its process, can make the exercise come to an immediate end.

For these reasons, the exercises need to be done every day so that you see all these obstacles for yourself and know what to do. In this way, with daily practice you learn more about how to do it. Astral projection demands patience and persistence. You need to be prepared to learn from each attempt you make and explore further into the exercise. Then the results will happen seemingly by themselves, sometimes without you expecting it at all.

SUMMARY OF WEEK 2 EXERCISES

These are the exercises to practice this week:
1. Being aware of what you are doing during the day.
2. Concentration/visualisation on an object.
3. Astral projection by concentrating upon the heart.

Also, continue with the two from last week:
1. Relaxation – do it before practicing projection.
2. Remembering dreams.

You need to be doing all the exercises given so far each day to succeed properly in the Astral. Persist with all these exercises on the course with determination, without giving up. Look into the obstacles that you face and continue until you overcome them. Sometimes this is quite difficult; nevertheless, with determination and persistence you will succeed.

Some people are able to achieve the Astral quicker than others are, but long it takes, keep going until you get it, because it is well worth the effort.

Here are some variations on the relaxation technique from last week that you can try:

1. Relax all the muscles of the body in one go, that is, let all the muscles of the whole body go loose at the same time. You can try again and again if you need to until you feel you are relaxed. Although this type of relaxation is pretty fast, it really relaxes the whole body straight away.

2. Relax each muscle of the body by tensing each muscle slightly and then immediately letting it go loose. You go through the whole body this way, paying attention to parts of the body that could be tense.

~

QUESTIONS AND ANSWERS

Astral Projection

Q. Are factors like noise (young kids), position of sleep, sharing a bed, age, linked to your ability to Astral travel?

A. Noise and sharing a bed can distract you, but if there is no alternative, you have to get used to it so that you do not notice it. The position of sleep is the one that you find works best or is practical, but lying on the back works best for most people. Age makes no real difference, it only exists here but children are less burdened by their egos than adults are. As one becomes more involved and caught up with life, one gets more asleep psychologically. However, this can be reversed and the ability to travel can be increased beyond what it was in childhood.

Since I have started this course, I have "tried" Astral travel a few times. The closest I got was a sense of a small, deep, black kind of void in front of my closed eyes. This seemed to get larger / deeper filling the whole room. As this happened I would feel (rather than hear) "flashing lights". However, I would still be aware of things like the TV on or my kids playing in another room. In fact, if anything, I would be even more aware of these distractions. Then everything would go back to normal. Does this sound as if I am on the right track? In addition, when trying this I was very aware of my breathing, which rather distracted me - should you breathe deep or shallow?

By learning to concentrate on the exercise, you will forget about the distractions. You should also forget about the breathing if you are not using it to project.

In your relaxation exercise, approximately how long should you spend relaxing your muscles?

You spend whatever time it takes to relax your muscles, which is normally about 5 minutes once you learn to do it properly.

I have been trying to Astral travel several times now and I can feel myself getting close. I have even had some of the experiences mentioned in the lecture. However, before I get anywhere I lose concentration on my heart either, because my heart rate becomes shallower and it is difficult to concentrate on it or I become distracted by my own breathing. Can you please give me some advice on what to do?

It helps to imagine the heart, and then you can stay focused on it better. With practice, you do not lose it like this.

Once you feel the heart beat, then visualise and concentrate on the heart, forgetting about the breathing; let it return to normal. If you think about breathing at any time, go straight back to the heart. Eventually with some practice, the distraction from the breathing will subside. It is a small ego that is affecting you.

If my daughter had not woken me - what are the chances that I would even remember the experience I had in the Astral?

If you are doing the retrospective exercise with your dreams, you would have a better chance of remembering it, but it is still possible not to realise that it has happened when you wake up in the morning. The lucid dream usually ends in two ways, you either merge into a dream, in which case you have to remember it when you next wake up, or you go back to your body, whether woken up by something in the physical or not.

I have tried to Astral project numerous times still with no success. I can relax my body to the point where my body is tingling, almost as if it has fallen asleep, like what happens when you sit on your foot for a long time, after that, nothing. Sometimes, this feeling gets really severe and my body feels like it is contorted into odd positions, even though I am just lying on my back. This is also hard to explain. One time, while I was trying to project, I was in steady relaxation for about 15 minutes and during the other five minutes my body felt like it was sideways even though I was lying on my back. Is this my Astral body moving or am I doing something wrong? Are there any dietary precautions I should be taking? I have the same problem with the heartbeat being too faint and becoming obscure because of the breathing. Should breathing

be a conscious effort? I mean 1...2...3...4 Hold...1...2...3...4...
When you Astral project, how conscious are you of the experience? Would Astral projecting be as conscious as being in the physical body?

Once you relax, you need to concentrate on the exercise without paying attention to the sensations that are happening.

When your body felt like it was sideways even though you were lying on your back, your Astral body had already split. This was your Astral body moving, although other parts of the Astral body can also move separately from the physical body. Next time, slowly get up from the bed and you can find yourself in the Astral. You were not doing anything wrong - you were very close.

As far as dietary precautions go, the main thing is not to eat a heavy meal before you sleep.

When the heartbeat becomes too faint and obscure, you should visualize it and you will find it again. Once you do, and then return to normal breathing. With practice, you do not lose it like this.

When you Astral project you are conscious of the experience, just as conscious as being in the physical body. However there can be times when it is a bit dreamlike, but these are the exceptions.

Could I have projected and taken off in flight even though trying to move at the time was impossible? I have also flown before by the way. It is one of the most exhilarating experiences. You come away feeling 10 years younger and oh so relaxed.

Yes, you could have eventually projected and taken off in flight. Normally if you cannot move, you just wait a little longer and you drift up a bit and can get out. Alternatively, you could try to see if you could get out by rolling over on your side, then out of bed. However, struggling and sharp movements can easily wake you up in the physical.

Sometimes, when trying the exercise, I start feeling heaviness, almost pressure in my head. I start feeling as if I am being tilted in a circular motion and I feel dizzy. I can carry on, but I have never got beyond this and I never feel as if I have fallen asleep. Am I doing the exercise correctly? In addition, can you concentrate on breathing because sometimes breathing blocks the feeling of the heart beating?

If you feel as though you are being tilted and are moving in a circular motion, and if this is quite noticeable, you can try slowly getting up from the bed to see if you are in the Astral. You may just catch the moment after you have split. However, if you are not quite there, it is important to concentrate on the exercise you are doing. Focusing the mind will bring about the split.

If you are concentrating on the heart, forget about the breathing. Let it go on normally and stay just with the heart. You can concentrate on the breathing alone as an exercise if you want to experiment with that, but remember to stick just to that, don't switch between it and the heart or anything else, or you may easily spoil the exercise.

I tried relaxing my body. The heartbeat was there and I could feel it even shake the bed in rhythm. When I tried to project... nothing. Am I asleep when this happens or am I in that in-between stage of sleep and awake? Maybe I am trying too hard.

It is not that you are trying too hard, but you are getting too physically involved with the heartbeat. You will not then be able to sleep and sleep is needed for the projection (watch you do not get emotionally involved either, with tension for example).

Make sure you carry out the relaxation exercise first of all, then concentrate on the heartbeat, but relax into it. Try also to visualise the heart a bit more when you do it. You may find that other exercises like mantras help you to relax more into the projection, until you learn more about how it works.

Do not give up on the heartbeat though because with a bit more practice you could get somewhere with it. It can take a lot of patience and persistence to get it.

We are in that in-between stage of sleep and wakefulness when the splitting of the Astral and physical bodies takes place. As soon as you have projected, the physical body is asleep.

How do you know when it is the right time to try to get up and travel?

If you notice that the Astral body is moving about or parts of it is body are moving: the face, the leg rises up, the hands or fingers are moving etc; then take a chance and get up gently and naturally. When you get up, jump almost convinced it is the Astral so that you can fly. Then you will prove where you are.

Sometimes you just rise up a little way and you may not feel as though you have projected, but you also need to get up to check. Other times though the projection is obvious, or you already find yourself in the Astral.

I keep practicing the exercise, except I place my hands on my chest to better feel my heart beat. Should I do this? Also, my heart does beat faster and faster, but then it feels like I have to fight to breathe, which usually breaks my concentration. What should I do?

First of all, you need to get your hands off your chest, because it is distracting you and you are becoming too involved with it.

Secondly, as you start the practice, relax and go gently into the practice. When you begin to feel your heart beating, carry on as though your heart has always been beating in this way and keep your concentration on the practice. Then, you will feel the first signs of Astral projection.

However, once the signs appear again you need to be concentrated in the practice and not get involved in what is happening. This is very important, because either with your excitement or your fear, you get stuck at one point or the exercise will come to an end.

Keep going - you are not very far from achieving it.

I just tried the heart beat exercise. I asked for divine help to keep my mind clear and focused, to keep evil away, and to assist me in projection. I lay down and relaxed my body twice. Then I focused on my breathing. First, I felt the beating in my ears. Then my feet up to my calves tingled and the tips of my hands. Then I was hearing the beating in my chest. Then I felt this circular motion in the centre of my chest near my heart, my feet and my hands. Then I only remember waking up, I did not get to the jumping part. How am I progressing? What was this? Was it just in my mind or what? Should my eyes be open or closed?

Yes, you are getting there; you were splitting into the Astral when you woke up.

Try to keep going with the exercise no matter what is starting to happen to you due to the splitting. Watch out for emotions too because they can easily wake you up.

You should have your eyes closed, sleep will arrive better and you are less likely to be distracted.

How do you know when to stop concentrating on your heartbeat and when you are out of your body?

When you actually lift up out of your body, when part of your Astral body moves independently of the physical one, or when you have gone through the stages of projection and feel paralysed.

When I am trying to Astral travel, I get all these sensations, my mind is fully awake and I feel that my body is dense and unable to move. Am I supposed to fall asleep and then wake up? I have been unable to Astral travel.

You will do better to pay less attention to the sensations and to concentrate upon the exercise, regardless of what sensations are taking place.

You also need to forget that you are falling asleep. Just relax and make sure that there is no anxiety or tension; you can often feel that you are still awake when you have actually projected. So continue with your exercise until there are definite signs of projection itself.

Since I heard in the lesson about concentrating on the heartbeat, I have practiced that nearly every day. In the evening I always fall asleep, so I practiced it in the afternoon, which gave me some more results, but I only got some of the first things you describe - peep in the ear and feeling heavy. Are there any other techniques, which are a little more effective?

It sounds as though if you keep continuing with this one you will get some results. There are exercises that suit some people better than others however and as you go along the courses, you will get different ones. It is a matter of trying them and being very patient.

I enjoy the lectures a lot and especially the last one. It led me immediately to an Astral travel experience again, the best and most convenient one I have had. It was my first, but short flight. I have

been practicing one year now to consciously project and my efforts were somewhat forced, uncomfortable, experiments. I have had many questions, trying to solve all of them by myself, which is not easy. Therefore, I consider this course truly precious. The questions that have been torturing me mostly are:

1. What kept me mostly worried was the lack of control. Why don't I have control of the movement of the Astral body? In the first months, it was very difficult to move the Astral body; I was mostly floating above the physical body. Only after one year did I start walking a little and flying, and spending more time in the Astral

2. Why can't I see clearly?

3. What are the reason and the purpose of those loud sounds, which resemble the sound of birds flying? The grosser the sounds the more painful and difficult it was to detach from the Astral body. I remember once after a projection I had no strength to move for half an hour. Also, I feel strange sensations on the body, as if streams of something are flowing, especially on the side of the neck and at the base of the spine (a very uncomfortable push). Sometimes it feels as if the Astral body rises slowly upwards and sometimes it feels as if it withdraws from the lower to the higher parts of the body and then leaves through the head.

4. A common problem was that I was getting stuck in the body and only a few parts detaching. It is a real struggle to detach completely.

5. It is very very confusing that when I walk in the Astral through the house I open the doors normally. How is it possible for the Astral arms to touch and open the material doors? Doors, which are closed in the physical, seem to be open, and vice versa.

6. When is the best time to Astral project? Usually, I am a little scared to project in the night (perhaps a childhood fear of darkness) so I project during the day, which can be done only during holidays though. In the night I see very poorly, which is a problem. On the other hand I wonder how I see and perceive the light, since the Astral eyes don't function with the light as the physical ones do.

Is there any way to perceive the places and objects more clearly, with more light? I guess not, it is a rather stupid question, but please tell me your opinion on it.

1. It is because you need to increase your level of consciousness. This will increase with the exercises on the course and the whole esoteric work. It also improves with experience.
2. Again, it is due to the level of consciousness, but it can also be due to interference from an ego or an outside entity. If this happens again use a conjuration (another topic) then you will see clearer if this was the problem.
3. You need to be less identified with the sensations of the body. There are symptoms, but the egos can exaggerate them. It is better to stick to the exercise you are doing (for example, if you are on the heart, concentrate just on that, or a mantra, etc.) until the moment you are out. Even if you are coming out, do not get identified with what is happening or the sensations - continue the exercise. Yes, you can go out either way.
4. If a few parts of the body detach, slowly and naturally get up because the split has already taken place.
5. You can open the doors because they are in the Astral and are made of Astral matter, just as we can move things in the physical world with the physical body.
6. You can project at any time - you just need to sleep. Many people have great success with an afternoon nap because they are not too tired when they try. The night has its own advantages though; the atmosphere is quieter and more conducive to mystical things.

The fear is something that can be overcome. The Astral eyes see Astral things just as the physical ones see physical things. Clarity in the Astral is due to the level of consciousness, the interference of entities and what is being shown. The consciousness is woken up by spiritual beings when they need to teach or show something.

In general, I have always been a light sleeper and maybe that is why I am finding Astral projection difficult. What is the most important feature in reaching the Astral: the sleeping on the back,

listening to the heartbeat or the relaxation? I never sleep on my back but I am trying to train myself, also blocking outside noise, but I have not made much progress. Is the main part of listening to the heartbeat to block out the subconscious thoughts and day dreaming so that they do not mask the Astral?

You can be in any position that is comfortable. The thing that is most helpful in getting to the Astral is concentration. Concentrate fully on the exercise that you are doing. That is why it is important to practice concentration with the exercises on this course and to concentrate upon what you are doing during the day.

I have been doing the concentration on the heart beat exercise. All of a sudden, a rushing to the head feeling happens and then I feel like I am floating above my body. It is quite a pleasant, releasing feeling. I cannot see anything but black. I still have my eyes closed. Should I try opening them or will that break the exercise?

You should open your eyes when you reach that stage, because you have already gone into the Astral. It will only break the exercise if you do it before you split.

I am currently doing the course and had an interesting experience last week that has given me quite a lot to think about. I would appreciate your thoughts and any advice you may have regarding this matter.

Firstly, and quite fortunately, simple self-observation is something I have been practicing for over a year now and can appreciate how self-awareness here would translate to the Astral.

About 6 months ago, I recognised I was having recurring dreams. One night I was even able to "redirect" a dream by thinking "Nah uh. I am not going there tonight" and did not. These are not "bad" dreams or nightmares by the way.

After last week's lecture, when I went to bed I was beautifully relaxed, concentrating on my heartbeat. Suddenly I thought "[main content of dream]!" and at that instant the buzzing symptom began with great intensity. It was quite remarkable. (Although I am quite familiar with the buzzing sensation, I find it really uncomfortable and am trying to work through what I believe is fear, which prevents me from completely separating.)

I dislike the buzzing sensation so much that, in this instance, I put my fingers in my ears in an attempt to dull it. After a short period of this, I gently returned to my heartbeat, and with great hilarity realised that it was my Astral body with which I had tried to block my ears, etc!

To me, two issues stand out. 1 - The thought connection to a previous dream event that clearly became a trigger to commence separation, which has never occurred with me before, and 2 - (Although I haven't got to your lecture on Intuition) the feeling I get is there is something I need to learn further by dealing with this dream/issue in the Astral. (Even if it is to simply determine whether it is additional egos making mischief, but I actually suspect not).

Fear, avoidance and denial seem to be the obvious "egos" in this experience. So, if for the time being I set these aside, my curiosity and enthusiasm is fired, fear allayed, and I have room to develop more courage needed to actually separate. Hopefully with the potential to learn something, which I feel may just hold something of deep significant importance to me.

Thank you for providing simple access, and presenting this and other Gnostic matters with a responsible approach.

The decisions you make in the physical regarding what you are going to do in the Astral translate into the Astral that very night, so you find yourself doing or not doing them, depending on what you decided.

Concentration on the heart is a very powerful exercise. If you have been very relaxed and concentrating on your heartbeats, it is very likely that your concentration on the heart triggered off the steps for real Astral projection, to the point where you were out of your body, closing your Astral ears. You simply missed the separation as you may have drifted on and off from sleep. The dream you mention could not have triggered off that type of projection you experienced simply because, if you have projected with a dream, you would have found yourself within that dream immediately.

There is certainly a lot to learn from dreams; it is very good that you are using your intuition for your dreams. It could be the case that in that dream your are being shown aspects of yourself, or something that you need to be aware of, that is something only you can decipher with the help of your intuition and looking into your life as you live it.

Fear of the unknown is very common in life. There are many

things in life that were the subjects of our fear, but we got on with them and now we do not even remember to be afraid of them. Think of a piece of fruit that you do not know of, would you eat it? Your answer would be no, but a person who knows the fruit will eat it and even enjoy it with no thought of fear. It is your courage and determination to go through whatever you need to go through, to experience conscious Astral projection that will change your approach to your practices. You will see later on how much you will enjoy that wonderful feeling of actually leaving your body, so that when it will not happen you will long for it so much, simply because out there, there is so much to learn, so much to see, so much to experience for yourself!

I have tried to concentrate on my heart in both the lying and sitting positions but getting no joy. At moments, I can feel it ever so slightly flutter but mostly I cannot feel a thing. What am I supposed to be sensing? Am I supposed to be sensing anything? If however I hold my breath, I do feel it pounding in my chest. What should I do?

You need to be visualising the heart, even if you cannot feel it very well. The more you do this the more you will gradually begin to feel the heart. Later on, you will feel your heart as soon as you concentrate on it. Getting visualisation right is the key to it. Maintaining the visualisation will enable you to project with this technique.

It is important to practice visualisation for at least 10 minutes a day; the more you do it the more you will explore your heart and get interested in what the heart is esoterically. Visualisation will also help you in any other Astral exercise that you do, because you learn to focus the mind

Week 3

Waking Up in Dreams

WAKING UP IN DREAMS

In this topic, we are going to look at a simple technique through which you can become conscious in the Astral by waking up in a dream. With it, you can carry out exactly the same investigations in the Astral as you would when you project from your bed.

In the normal course of sleep, dreams occur in the Astral plane; therefore, it is possible to become conscious of being there while in a dream. This happens to many people and it is commonly called "lucid dreaming".

However, there is a difference between a dream and being conscious in the Astral. When dreaming, there is no recognition of being in a dream; it just happens and there is no self-awareness to enable us to realise where we are. When you are conscious in a dream however, you know that you are in a dream, and then you are conscious in the Astral. This is why we use the term "waking up in dreams" rather than "lucid dreaming."

There are exercises that can be done to become conscious in the Astral while dreaming. They basically involve questioning during the day to see whether you are in the Astral or in the physical world in order to record that question in the subconscious. You then repeat it while dreaming and thereby realise that you are there.

The things that are done during the day naturally become recorded in the subconscious. The subconscious then projects what it has recorded onto the Astral which, combined with what is actually there, become the scenes that form the dreams. In most cases, they seem real to the dreamer, but they are more often just the dreamer's own creation.

Everything that exists here actually has its counterpart in the Astral. Every physical form has its Astral form, because things are multidimensional. Therefore, if we were awake in that dimension, we could see our house, town, friends etc but in a dream, it is mostly altered. Even when we do wake up in the Astral, we can often see what is there, but occasionally the dream images continue, due to the projections of the subconscious.

If during the day, therefore, you repeatedly ask yourself where you are, whether you are in the physical world or in the Astral, that questioning is eventually recorded in the subconscious, and you will eventually ask it at night while in a dream. Then, in the dream, you can realise that you are in the fifth dimension.

That dimension has different laws than here as we can fly and move through objects. If we question ourselves here using things that only occur in the fifth dimension, for example flying, then we know what dimension we are in if they happen.

There are two main things to use to check where you are: jumping and pulling your finger. The first involves jumping slightly in the air, with the serious intention of floating or flying. Obviously, we are not going to fly here, but if we do it in the Astral then we will fly. If you do that enough here, you will begin to do it in dreams, then when you jump and you actually float or fly, you can easily realise where you are and be conscious in the Astral.

When you practice this, you do not need to jump very high, just slightly. You do however need to seriously question where you are and whether you are in the physical world or in the Astral. It is important to do this questioning sincerely, really asking yourself the question. If you do it and you think that you are really in the physical world, you will jump in the dream but you will think that you are in the physical and it will not work. You may just land straight back down or you may fly convinced that you are in the physical. You also need to do it really with the feeling that you are going to fly. When you have flown a few times in the Astral, you know how that feels.

The second check you can make is to question and pull your finger at the same time. In the Astral, matter is different, so if we pull our finger there it stretches. This is useful when we want to check where we are but when it would be inappropriate to jump up in the air, however discreetly (you do not want to look like an idiot bounding around the office for example).

To make all this questioning work, it is important to do it very frequently, to be checking often during the day. Eventually this will become recorded and you will start to do it in your dreams.

When you question, it is best to do it with awareness, looking around carefully at the place you are in, the objects around you, etc.

You need to genuinely question where you are, actually doubt and wonder. If you don't, when you question in the dream, you can be convinced that you are in the physical world. Even to the extent of jumping up into the air, floating and wondering how you could float in the physical, or thinking that you can float in the physical. This has happened to me and to many students very often.

I used things to trigger off the remembrance of jumping by jumping whenever I saw certain things, knowing that whenever I saw those things in a dream I would be likely to question where I was and jump. I used to help myself to remember to jump by jumping every time I saw the stars at night, then I would often be helped to wake up by being shown the night sky in a dream.

Strange things that you see sometimes can also be used to remind you to question where you are because strange things happen very often in dreams. You might be looking into the night sky and see UFOs flying around for example. Whenever you see something strange or unusual, then use it to question whether you are in the physical world or in the Astral world, then either pull your finger or jump to check.

Once in a dream I saw a spiritual Master called Rabolu in front of me. He jumped up in the air doing somersaults. I thought that it just could not happen and realised that I was in the Astral. In fact, I woke up in the Mental plane, which is a higher plane than the Astral, but still in the fifth dimension.

I have been in the Astral on different occasions and have met students who were in a dream. I remember asking one to wake up and jump, I told him that he was in the Astral, but he could only partially recognise me because of the dream images that he had. I jumped and floated but it made no difference, he was too asleep on that occasion. He may have remembered seeing me in a dream if he had done the exercise to remember dreams when he woke up in the morning.

When a person dreams they can look like people who we see here drunk or on drugs to someone who is awake in the Astral.

THE IMPORTANCE OF AWARENESS

This technique works best when using the awareness throughout the day, because awareness makes the consciousness active. The clearer the level of your consciousness is in daily life, the clearer and more lucid will be the dreams you have.

Awareness makes it easier to see what is going on in dreams and thereby makes it easier to remember to question where you are. Therefore, you can make better use of the opportunities to wake up there.

The consciousness cannot only be activated, but the amount of consciousness can be increased, which is very important. To increase the amount of consciousness you have, you will need to learn the techniques in the Self Knowledge and Esoteric courses. These techniques include alchemy which gives lucidity to the consciousness, and techniques to see and eliminate subconscious states such as fear, anger, various mental images, etc, which we call egos and which make up the subconscious. These keep each person in a daydream throughout daily life. That daydream continues when sleep arrives and becomes dreams. In this esoteric work, explained on another course, you learn to eliminate those subconscious elements and to increase the amount of consciousness. I will explain more about dreams and the subconscious in another topic on this course.

For now however, work with awareness and in doing so, this exercises and feeds the consciousness that you have. It is a matter of getting out of the daydream and "waking up" to where you are in the present moment. If you catch yourself daydreaming, go back to what you are doing immediately so that you cause the consciousness to wake up.

The more you can practice being aware of where you are and what you are doing the better. Combine this with questioning which dimension you are in and you have a very effective means of getting to the Astral plane.

～

WEEK 3 EXERCISES

These weekly exercises are most important for getting into the Astral. If you do them all methodically each day this week you will have a much better chance of being able to succeed than if you just try a mix of things here and there.

Exercise 1

To wake up in dreams

1. **Questioning where you are** - Ask whether you are in the physical world or in the Astral world by using the jump and pulling your finger, and see if there is anything strange around you in the ways that I have described above. Remember to genuinely question, looking around you with as much awareness as you can. Try it as often as you can.

2. **Practicing Awareness** - Be aware during the day. Help this exercise to work by making sure you try to be aware when you do the three things I mentioned last week: washing yourself, putting your shoes on and eating.

3. **Practicing Awareness and Questioning** - Go for a walk for 10-15 minutes each day and intensively practice being aware. Practice questioning which dimension you are in by pulling the finger and jumping.

Exercise 2

To Astral Project

1. **Continue your concentration on the heart** - Experiment this week with the different methods of visualising the heart to see which is most effective for you and to learn the different ways of visualising. You should make use of this time to learn to concentrate on the heart, because we will be using other techniques soon and you will lose the opportunity to learn this technique if you don't make use of it now.

2. **Visualising an object for ten minutes each day** - Vary the objects and continue with 10 minutes each day.

Exercise 3

To Remember Dreams

Lie still when you wake up, go back over the night's dreams and use the mantra Raom Gaom.

QUESTIONS AND ANSWERS

Q. How do you know the difference between Astral projecting and waking up in a dream?

A. When dreaming we are not self-aware so we cannot say, "this is a dream", but when we are in the Astral, we can. We know that we are in that plane, just as we know that we are in the physical plane now. The difference is only in the way that you get into the Astral.

With projection, you go straight from the body. When you wake up in a dream, you have missed the projection but you are still conscious in the Astral. You can be in the same place from both methods. It is only the way that you get there that is different.

I am not sure if this was Astral projection. At first when I went to sleep at about midnight or so, I was dreaming already, then I realised I was lucid dreaming. I kept on trying to get out of my body and I started feeling pains...in my dream. I lost that and I started dreaming again. This time I was lying down in bed trying to project because I knew I was dreaming. Suddenly I popped out of my body and I was just floating in the air in some brightly lit sky somewhere. I then tried to will myself to go into my sister's bedroom but it felt like I was being pulled there. The candles in her room allowed me to see her dresser but that was all. After that brief pull, I was pulled outside of my house and it was just me and the night sky. Then I suddenly found myself in my body again at 12:30am.

Please tell me if this was Astral projection. I am so positive that it was because I have never experienced anything like this before. I partly doubt my experience as being a projection because I did not get to have what people call spherical vision. Maybe that comes with practice. I have been thinking about it all day so any feedback is appreciated.

Yes, you were in the Astral. When you are pulled to a place like that, it is generally because you need to be shown or experience something there. When a Master is called in the Astral there is also that pull.

Forget about having spherical vision or trying to perceive in a certain way. That can make you create things from your own imagination that are not really there and that can make you lose the Astral, turning it into a dream or bringing you back to the body. It just becomes a distraction; it is best to be simple and clear in the Astral.

There are different faculties and senses that enable us to perceive what we cannot see with the eyes, but you really need to develop them here in the physical world.

Just try to be aware while you are there, then any faculties will be naturally activated.

Can whatever you wish for happen in the Astral?

It is not the case that whatever you wish for happens in the Astral. You can however imagine things in the Astral and they will appear. They don't really exist there though, they are projections of the mind and with them, you can soon fall into a dream and lose awareness of the Astral. It is better to be clear of those projections so that you can actually see what is there.

I read about the ability to become anything like a room or a flame, or a chair. Do these things happen in the Astral or is that something else?

You can imagine things in the Astral and they become real, but it is not advisable because then you don't see things as they are and you can miss teachings.

Just how much practicing did you do before you finally did it. I cannot seem to get there with these exercises. I have projected before but it happened accidentally. I am starting to think I am doing something wrong. Is it because I am too tired when I do try? Have you all been falling asleep then waking up in the Astral? I need some help. Any hint at all would be appreciated. Thanks.

I had been developing awareness for six months before I tried Astral projection. I did not know about the Astral before then, but because of all that training in awareness I managed to project first time.

So far, we have given just one basic exercise for projection, but there are more. It can take a lot of practice, time and patience to do the things necessary to achieve the Astral.

Try doing the "jumping" exercise and pulling your finger during the day to get yourself to wake up in a dream. It is a very simple and effective exercise. If you are too tired, you can have difficulties projecting as the mind finds it difficult to focus and sleep arrives too quickly. The remedy is to conserve your energies by being less in the egos during the day and to go to bed when you are not so tired.

In my experience I tend to "wake up from dreams" either before the "split" or after. Is it normal to have dreams before the split?

You can have dream images before the split. You are getting into the Astral but you are missing the process of projection.

Opening my eyes ended two of my experiences in the Astral. Should I not do this in future?

Yes, you can open your eyes without losing the Astral, but try not to be absorbed in what you see. You should watch your egos in the Astral because feeling nervous and the like can bring you back to your body.

I think I did it! When I was dreaming, I suddenly thought, "Am I dreaming" I then realised that I was. I felt suddenly happy and free like I do when I am trying the awareness exercises in the daytime. However as soon as I realised it, my body started feeling fuzzy and vibrating. The place where I was dreaming disappeared and I felt as if I was waking up. I panicked because I thought I was seeing my room and my eyes were opening, so I told myself to keep in the dream. Then I must have fallen asleep again. Was this waking up in dreams? Why did I then wake up properly and how can I stop this?

Yes, you did wake up in a dream. It often only lasts for a short time as it did for you, then you wake back up in the physical world or lose self-awareness in the Astral and merge back into a dream. This is usually due to a lack of awareness and consciousness, although heightened emotional states such as panic can also bring you back to the body. It helps if you can hold on to Astral matter while you are there and to stay as naturally aware as possible, eliminating any egos (emotional states for example) that arise.

OK, I woke up in my dream and I thought, "hey, this is a dream, wow, now I should be able to do whatever I want". Therefore, I tried, but nothing happened. Is it possible that I didn't actually wake up but just dreamt that I did and so couldn't do what I wanted? Or is there something you have to do before you can actually do what you want or Astral project?

You did wake in your dreams, but the idea you have about Astral projection threw it out.

What you really need to do and should have done is investigate that plane and seek knowledge there. If you improve internally and become more conscious, then you can learn things that you can't even imagine at this moment, because the mind is a basic tool in comparison with what you can know through consciousness. Otherwise, you will be wasting your time there.

If you wake in your dreams again try finding out how that dimension works. For example, what happens if you jump, are things as solid as they are in the physical plane? Then try to push through something that is solid and then you will see for yourself what happens. Learn to investigate things, and then you will not go wrong.

I knew I was not in the Astral but I thought that lucid dreams were the ones where you could make anything happen. When I did jump in the dream I started to fly and then I woke up.

Lucid dreaming is an unclear term. When you know you are in a dream then an experience is taking place in the Astral plane. Don't waste the opportunity by trying to make things happen, you will only see what is in your subconscious if you do. Rather try to be aware of what is there. It will help you to stay out longer too.

A week ago, I saw something strange when I was driving and for a split second I thought was dreaming. That night while dreaming I was driving and I again saw something strange (a distortion of the windscreen). I thought that if I could concentrate on the distortion I would see what was really there. At this point I realised I was in the Astral but it was short lived. As I was driving in the dream, when I woke I thought I may have been driving in reality and nodded off at the wheel. I panicked to find my body to make sure it was still okay ... whoosh, back in my body, which of

course was sleeping in bed – it is still a start.

Yes, that is a good start. Don't forget to pull your finger and jump in the day; this will increase the chances of waking up in the Astral.

Lately I have tried to be more aware in my everyday life, focusing on seeing things in the present time rather than being with thoughts or emotions. In doing this I have realised I am remembering more of my dreams when I sleep and I am seeing more déjà vu scenarios of dreams or places I feel I have been before.

One night about a week and a half ago, towards the early hours in the morning (still dark outside), I felt I woke up within my dream state. This was quite unusual, but what made it more unusual was that as I woke within my dream I could see a dark shape, something I cannot really specify. It was about 20cm in height and 5cm in width and outside of this dark shape was a number of different rainbows like colours. In this state of mind, while I was sleeping, I felt this was the stage for me to try to Astral travel. I tried to leave my body and as soon as I tried, I snapped back into my body and was wide-awake. I later learned I should have probably not willed myself out of my body but let things take place by themselves. I would like to know from someone experienced if this sounds like the right process for Astral travel or was I in dreamland seeing things. If that was a complete and utter load of nonsense, could someone explain to me what might have happened?

By waking up within a dream state, you were already in the Astral. There is no need to try to leave the body if you become self-aware in a dream. You should have tried jumping to make sure you were there.

If you see anything strange like that object again, use the conjurations, which will be given later in the course. You will be able to get rid of any kind of negative influence or entity and you will be (along with your intuition) able to tell if something is good or is negative.

If you have just gone into the Astral, don't try to will yourself out of your body - actually get up slowly. As it was, you were just pulled back into it.

On the first day of the exercise, I asked myself a bunch of times if I was in the Astral or physical world. Last night I woke up, and decided to try to project again, which I do every night. This time I did project, but instead of walking outside of my house, it was a house in the country. I thought that I must be in a dream, but conscious. Therefore, I started walking when I realised something as if a magnetic force was pulling me towards something. A police officer told me which way to go and pointed. It was not necessary for her to do this as I was already going in that direction. I came upon three or four people as I was floating by and asked where I was going. They said, "Toward and through the crosses." I said thanks and proceeded to go further but I woke up.

Was this a test for me to try to accomplish or is this something I need to figure out on my own, since it was in the dream part of the Astral?

You were being taught in an experience.

When you are being pulled with a magnetic force like that it usually indicates that you are being led to a certain place. The police officers usually represent agents of the divine law, who are associated with Karma, just as the physical ones here are to a country's law.

If the crosses were like graves, they could mean death, but the cross has a meaning - the responsibility and sacrifice of the esoteric work, and also the alchemy.

You need to look at the particular experience and see what it means overall.

What role does the cosmic fire play in the Astral jump? Do I have to use it or is there no need to use the cosmic fire? I am really concerned about how dangerous it can be.

There are many kinds of cosmic fire. The one we mostly refer to is called the Kundalini. It has to be awakened first with the true esoteric work, although many mistakenly think it is easy and give wrong techniques to try to awaken it. Once it has been awakened, there is no danger from it.

You will do best to continue trying the Astral at this stage and not to worry about the cosmic fire. That will be explained on the Esoteric course.

I have had a couple of experiences where I was in a normal dream, and all of a sudden noticed something really unusual realising "hey, I am dreaming". On one occasion I quickly lost

control of the scene, and instead of being able to look at the images, they all became swirled together, and then I woke up. **Is control something that happens with practice? Or should I be doing something else to keep from losing the images and waking up? I am discovering with the exercises on awareness during the day that I am remembering more of the dreams that I do have during the night and am continuing to do the finger pulling/jumping exercises.**

It is a very common experience. What you need to watch is that you don't get too excited when you get into the Astral. If you keep working upon your emotions during the day, you will find in the future that the experiences will be clearer. Just keep persisting with it; you are on the right track. Keep learning and you will see that you are able to stay in the Astral for longer.

I was finally able to wake up in a dream after a day of relaxation exercises. I practiced the relaxation exercise and after a while, I fell asleep. When I woke up, I found myself in a city (I don't know where). I knew I was in a dream so I walked a few meters and I jumped with the will of flying and flew in the sky. A second after, I noticed a black bird that I passed and then fear arose in my whole body (although I am not afraid of a black bird in the physical plane). I hastily returned to my body by thinking of and moving my body parts. I noticed that the time in my dream was the same in the physical but only a little later.

It is very important to overcome the fear. This is done by gaining experience in the Astral, by learning to use the conjurations and by doing the esoteric work here. This includes the elimination of ego, states such as fear and, Alchemy, which transforms the energies. You get fear when the energies are weak but it goes away when they are strong. When you get the information on the conjurations, later in this course, if you see anything that makes you afraid again, you can conjure it. Then you will get the confidence that you can deal with things in the Astral plane.

Yes, it is true that time is different there than it is here, because we are in eternity when we are in the fifth dimension. Whenever you are shown the time in the Astral, you need to pay careful attention to it because the numbers of the time will give you an indication of how you are doing spiritually. There will also be more about this in another topic.

Week 4

Mantras for Astral Projection

MANTRAS FOR ASTRAL PROJECTION

For this session, we are going to study another technique for Astral projection, as concentration and visualisation are not the only ways to Astral project. It is also possible to project using mantras, although you will still need to concentrate upon the mantra.

Mantras are constantly repeated sounds, words or phrases. They can be used for a variety of purposes such as increasing intuition or for remembering dreams, etc. For this topic, I will mention mantras that are effective for Astral projection.

Three of the ones used here have an elongated pronunciation of vowels. Pronouncing the vowels like this stimulates the different chakras in the Astral body. Chakras are senses of the Astral body, there are seven of them and each, when stimulated, give their own different psychic effects. In this case, they help to detach the connections that exist between the physical and Astral bodies.

It is worth remembering that this pronouncing of mantras stimulates the chakras and helps the projection just for the time that you do it. If you don't pronounce the mantras, you are not going to get their benefits. However, when you do the spiritual work you can activate the chakras and their corresponding faculties fully and permanently.

PRONOUNCING THE MANTRAS

For Astral projection, we are going to use the following mantras and I am going to explain how to pronounce each of them. Have a listen to the sound files, if you have access to them, so that you are able to hear how the mantras are pronounced (links to the sound files are given in page 68)

La Ra S - pronounced, Laaaaaaaaaaa Rrraaaaaaaaaaa Sssssssssssssss.

La - The vowel 'a' is pronounced as the 'a' in the word 'far'.

Ra - The 'r' is trilled. The 'a' is pronounced as the 'a' in the word 'far'.

S - The 's' is pronounced as the 's' in snake, like a hiss.

Breathe in through the nose; breathe out slowly through the mouth pronouncing the syllable.

You use one breath for each of the syllables. For example, (breath) Laaaaaaaaaaa, (breath) Rrraaaaaaaaaaa, (breath) Sssssssssssssss.

Egypto - pronounced, Eeeeeeeeeeee hiiiiiiiiiiiiip toooooooooooo.

E - The vowel 'e' is pronounced as the 'e' in the word 'let'.

Hip - The vowel 'i' is pronounced as the 'ea' in the word 'tea', or the 'ee' in the word 'sheep'.

To - The vowel 'o' is pronounced as the 'o' in the word 'more'.

Breathe in through the nose; breathe out slowly through the mouth pronouncing the syllable.

You use one breath for each of the syllables. For example, (breath) Eeeeeeeeeeee, (breath) Hiiiiiiiiiiiiip, (breath) Toooooooooooo.

Fa Ra On - pronounced Faaaaaaaaaaa Rrraaaaaaaaaaa Ooooooooooonnnn.

Fa - The vowel 'a' is pronounced as the 'a' in the word 'far'.

Ra - The 'r' is trilled. The 'a' is pronounced as the 'a' in the word 'far'.

On - The vowel 'o' is pronounced as the 'o' in the word 'more'.

Breathe in through the nose; breathe out slowly through the mouth pronouncing the syllable.

You use one breath for each of the syllables. For example, (breath) Faaaaaaaaaaa, (breath) Rrraaaaaaaaaaa, (breath) Ooooooooooonnnn.

You can practice a variation of this mantra by visualising the Egyptian pyramids while you do it. One example of this mantra working is a student of this course who pronounced this mantra and woke up in the Astral inside one of the pyramids.

Tae re re re re re – This mantra is different to the three previous ones.

Tae - pronounced as in the word 'Thai' (the inhabitants of Thailand).

Re - pronounced as in the word 'rep.' (short for 'representative', as in 'sales rep.').

It is pronounced quickly, without elongating the vowels.

Tae is pronounced once, and then you pronounce the other five syllables one after the other very quickly. This mantra has a light singing tone to it. If you have access to them, listen to the sound files to get the tone of the mantra right.

This is all done in one breath and you continue repeating the whole mantra with each breath.

You can access the sound files for these mantras by typing the following addresses in your Internet browser:
  http://www.gnosticweb.org/astralbook/La_Ra_S.mp3
  http://www.gnosticweb.org/astralbook/Egypto.mp3
  http://www.gnosticweb.org/astralbook/Fa_Ra_On.mp3
  http://www.gnosticweb.org/astralbook/Tae_Re_Re.mp3

Pronounce these mantras until you Astral project or fall asleep. When you are pronouncing these mantras you still need to concentrate on them, they will be far less effective if you don't.

There are other mantras that can be used for Astral projection and you will come across those later if you continue with the courses. These will be enough to go on with for a while.

PROJECTING WITH THE MANTRAS

It is best to develop a certain mantra (such as La Ra Ssss for example) and try it for a few days in a row or longer. This will allow the chakras to activate more with the particular mantra, because some activate different chakras than others. Bear in mind that you can practice the Astral at any time of the day; the morning can be a particularly good time. When you choose a mantra, stick with it for the duration of the exercise; don't change to another mantra or to a different type of exercise during a practice.

Concentration upon pronouncing the mantras is important because if you don't have it you could lose track of the syllables you are pronouncing because they are interrupted by thoughts. Then you can forget where you are in the mantra and the continuity of it will be broken and disrupted and the exercise will be weakened.

Because these mantras work by stimulating the chakras, you will increase their effectiveness by practicing the mantra you are going to use for projection between ten minutes and an hour some time before you try to astral project. This will get the chakra spinning and partially activated, so that when you do your projection exercise you have the advantage of the activated chakra, which will help the projection a great deal.

When you use these mantras to project with, you need to be lying down ready to sleep, as you would when practising concentration for Astral projection. Relax the body, and then pronounce the mantra aloud for a short time. Get progressively quieter until you are only pronouncing it in your mind. From then on breathe as normal as you no longer need to take a deep breath to pronounce the mantra aloud. Continue pronouncing it over and over in your mind until sleep arrives.

If you cannot pronounce the mantra aloud at the beginning for any reason, pronounce it mentally from the beginning.

The process of going into the Astral with mantras is the same as with concentration with the electric-like current and so on. However, parts of the Astral body may more noticeably begin to detach from the physical body. For example, an arm or a leg may lift up, a hand or fingers may move, or your face may be in a different direction to the one you are lying in. When anything like this happens, you may not realise that the body has detached. I have known a student who was doing this exercise and was spinning around. He was wondering what was happening, but he did not realise, or the thought never occurred to him, that he was actually in the Astral. On the other hand, I have known of a student who realised about this when pronouncing mantras and Astral projected ten times in one night, repeating the mantra each time and getting up whenever a body part moved.

If any of these things happen, or you have begun to float and you think you might have projected, slowly get up from the bed (you need to do it gently or you can wake yourself up) or roll out of bed gently and check whether you are in the Astral, in the ways that I have mentioned in previous topics. If you are in the physical, go back to bed and try again. Once the signs appear again, get up. If you keep doing this, you will eventually get up in the Astral. However, you may also lift out of the body or wake up already in the Astral from pronouncing these mantras.

You need to train yourself to get up from bed when the parts of your body begin to move. Don't pretend or imagine that you are getting up; you have to actually get up from bed.

Like everything with Astral projection, a lot of patience is required and for some people it can take a long time. If you persist, you find that it will eventually work.

~

WEEK 4 EXERCISES

Although this is a technique to project using mantras, you still need to be able to concentrate upon the mantra. To go back to visualisation techniques (as we will soon do in future topics), you will need to have maintained your ability to concentrate upon what you are doing and to visualise. Therefore, we are going to continue with what is important to maintain and increase these while we use mantras.

These weekly exercises are most important for getting into the Astral. If you do them all methodically each day this week you will have a much better chance of being able to succeed than if you just try a mix of things here and there.

Exercise 1
To Astral Project

1. **Mantras** - Try two different ones this week starting with La Ra S. This will give you the opportunity to develop each one properly and to learn how each one works. They are all slightly different and each different sound has a different effect on the chakras. If you keep to a particular one for long enough you will activate that chakra much more, making the exercise more effective.

2. **Visualising an object for ten minutes each day** - Vary the objects, for example, a glass of water, a plant, flowers, etc and continue with at least ten minutes each day. Remember to close your eyes when you are recreating the object in your mind and to recreate it often. Don't try to stay there with your eyes open or force yourself to keep staring at the object for a long period of time. Gradually increase the time you spend on this exercise but begin with just a little.

Exercise 2
To Wake up in Dreams

1. **Questioning where you are** - Ask whether you are in the physical world or in the Astral world by using the jump, pulling your finger and by seeing if there is anything strange around you. Remember to genuinely question, looking around you with as much awareness as you can. Try it as often as you can.

2. **Practicing Awareness** - Be aware during the day. Help this exercise to work by making sure you try when you do the three things I mentioned last week –washing yourself, putting your shoes on and eating.

3. **Practicing Awareness and Questioning** - Go for a walk for 10-15 minutes each day and intensively practice being aware. Practice questioning which dimension you are in by pulling the finger and jumping.

Exercise 3

To Remember Dreams

Lie still when you wake up and go back over the night's dreams. Use the mantra Raom Gaom. When you pronounce this mantra you need to prolong the vowel "o" like RaaaOooooommm GaaaOooooommm.

∼

QUESTIONS AND ANSWERS

Q. **Part of the problem with the mantra is that I cannot pronounce it aloud. I think I will continue with the heart for the moment and wait for a few weeks until my wife is working nights to try mantras.**

In any one night, does it matter if I swap around between the heart and a mantra i.e. go to sleep concentrating on heart then wake up later and try a mantra?

In my home office, I have a comfortable armchair, which gives support to my back and neck. Is it possible to project while sitting relaxed in a chair and concentrating on the heart during the day? Sometimes I have the opportunity to try this but I just have not bothered to date because I thought it would not work.

A. It does not really matter if you swap around in one night between concentration and a mantra if you already have concentration. However, it will help to develop your concentration and your ability to experience the exercise if you concentrate on one for a while, because then you can learn more about it.

You can project from any position as long as you can concentrate on the exercise and can sleep, although lying on the back is the position that most people find works best.

I tried the exercise in the afternoon by saying the mantra tae re re re re re and I felt really heavy, swirling movements and a sense of dizziness. This increased when I visualised my Astral legs

moving etc. However, I then got up and I was still in the physical. I still felt the sensations quickly when I tried it again. **Am I getting close and is it ok to visualise the body separating? Am I trying to get up too quickly? should I leave it for a longer period?**

You are getting close, but you should not visualise the parts of the body moving. Just focus on the mantra and they can begin to move by themselves. Visualising the body moving is part of the same problem; it distracts you from focussing on the mantra and can disrupt the exercise.

You are trying to get up too quickly. You should leave it for a longer period of time; until either the body parts begin to move of their own accord, or until you begin floating upwards.

If there are three syllables in a mantra, do I sound each syllable in the same tone? Does it matter whether I do or not?

Yes, sound each syllable in the same tone. It will be evenly repetitive and will then work better.

In a previous lesson, you said that if you stop practicing the concentration exercise you would lose what you have built up very quickly. If I swap to using mantras for the next week or so will, I lose what I have built up from concentrating on the heart. Should I alternate nights, or do they compliment each other?

It is all right because you are still concentrating on the mantra, but continue with the concentration/visualisation exercises that are a preparation for the Astral. Try those at other times during the day and they will help to build up the concentration.

I have many periods during the day where I am free for 5-10 minutes (I can be sitting but not lying down). Is there any simple exercises you can recommend that will help me improve my awareness / ability to Astral project?

You can do a basic concentration/visualisation exercise that will keep your concentration going for the Astral. Look at an object carefully, then close your eyes and recreate the image in great detail. When you lose it, open your eyes again and repeat the process.

Seeing that I share a bed with my wife and she is a light sleeper (I don't think she will be too impressed if I wake her a few times a night getting up to see if I am in the Astral), is there any less obtrusive ways to check i.e. by pulling my finger when I am lying in bed? In addition, I will not be able to say the mantra aloud. Will this affect my ability to Astral project significantly?

You can try pulling your finger while you are still in bed to check. Wait for sure signs of projection before you try to get up in the Astral. Saying the mantra mentally still works, it is just a bit more difficult.

In regards to the relaxation exercise, do I just systematically go through my muscles telling them to relax in my head?

Don't tell the muscles to relax in your head, feel each muscle relaxing. Experiment with the three ways of relaxing the muscles that I mention in the topics so that you find what suits you best.

If I am doing a mantra exercise during the day, I assume I should keep my eyes closed. Would it be of benefit to wear an "eye cover" to block out light? Will the concentration on the heart exercise work equally well in the daytime?

It is best to close your eyes, but there is no need to wear a light block unless you find the light a problem. If you are concentrating on the mantra, it will not matter if its daylight. It is the same for concentration on the heart; it will also work in the daytime.

You said to visualise pyramids for "Fa Ra On". I am going to use "La Ra S" (I like the sound of it) Is there anything I should visualise for this one to make it more effective? When you say to concentrate on them, do you mean to concentrate on how they sound or to concentrate on the "feelings" they invoke?

You do not have to visualise pyramids for "Fa Ra On" - it is just an option. It is best not to visualise anything with "La Ra S". You just concentrate on doing them without thinking about how they sound or feel.

Can anyone tell me what it means to trill the 'r' in the Mantra "La Ra S"? My first language is French, so does it mean to roll the 'r' as we do in French?

I think it would be like the French, but I don't know exactly how that is pronounced. The 'r' is trilled in many languages, although I am not familiar with most of them. I know that it is trilled in Welsh and in some Arabic languages.

I have been using the mantras now every night since I received the lesson. The first night I felt like my foot twisted up and started to wiggle about, but I don't think it was my actual foot, as I didn't seem to feel any resistance from the bed covers. The second night I felt my thumb suddenly jump up as well, then I felt the sensation in my feet disappear and this slowly worked its way up though my legs, then my hands and up my arms. Does all this sound normal? Am I on the right track?

The itching feeling on my face and other places, like my back and neck, what is that? I try to restrain from scratching but it just gets too much and I cannot focus on the heart when it happens.

In addition, I cannot seem to stay still when I wake up, I always move. Any advice on how I can stop moving first thing in the morning?

Yes, it is normal and you are on the right track, but when your foot twisted up and your thumb suddenly jumped up, you should have slowly got up, because the bodies had already split.

The itching is highlighted by an ego. If you go back to concentrating on the exercise, it will reduce and go away. You will then find at future times it is not there or goes away easily. Ignore it.

The body is trained with practice. Just keep going and eventually you will get there.

I was just wondering, when I projected before, or at least when I know I have projected, I have my vision and my head is out. However, with the foot and thumb thing, everything was dark, like my eyes were still closed. If I were to get up at this point what would happen? Would I get my sight? It feels like the bottom half of my body is out but the top half is still in the physical is that possible?

If you got up at that point, you could have projected, even though it was dark, because the bodies were already separating. It may or may not still be dark; it often depends on your state.

If you get into the Astral and its dark, you can use something to clear it called a conjuration, which I will explain about later on this course.

I have found that when I do any of the concentration practices in order to project, after a while, I get absolutely freezing feet! I never experience cold feet at any other time except when I am practicing these Astral exercises and the longer I do the exercise, the colder they get. It has got to the point where I have to wear ski socks every time I do a practice and my feet are still cold! Has anyone else experienced this? Do you know why this might be?

Yes, the body gets colder as we fall asleep. We normally do not notice it, but if we try to Astral project, we go much further into the process of sleep and we are aware of the increasing cold. I suppose too that some are more affected than others are.

I don't have a clue if I am saying the mantras at the right speed or tone.

The ones with elongated vowels are pronounced slowly for as long as each breath lasts.

I think I had my first experience, but I am not sure. It scared me to death though. I was lying on my side saying the mantras aloud and when I felt deeply relaxed, I started saying them to myself. The heartbeat was really noticeable too. I felt myself trying to roll over and get up but at the same time I was scared, yelling "no" and for someone to help me! It was as if a force was pulling at me but the fear I felt was unbelievable. I even found myself trying to grab my hubby's arm beside me to keep from leaving my body. Then I woke up. Was I almost there or was this something else? I have never experienced anything like this before. I was aware of everything during all this. Also, I read that once you have the ability to project, you can visit any place you want to go and even go to see loved ones that live far away. Is this true?

Yes, you were there. You had split and were leaving your physical body. If you had not been, so afraid you would have gone right out into the room in the Astral. You learn eventually that there is nothing to be afraid of although the fear of the unknown can be strong in the beginning. Fear generally is what we call an "ego". If you learn how to get rid of them, then this, combined with Alchemy, (both in future courses) will gradually remove fear.

Once you are in the Astral, through whatever means, you can travel to most places by visualising them.

I read the topic and practiced the mantra Egypto. I have been doing it for one week now before going to bed with only little results - that was until last night. As I was doing the mantras Egypto, I fell asleep, then I woke up and realised that I was separating from my body. It seemed like I was in some sort of weird trance. I was conscious and was having trouble separating from my body. I was reaching and pulling on anything I could, scared and confused. I forgot everything I was taught in the previous lessons about how to handle these situations.

The thing that scared me the most was that, before my eyes, a big teddy bear appeared sitting in my chair. It turned and looked at me. This scared me so much that I screamed to myself to wake up! It took a little while but I eventually woke up scared. I was not scared because something threatened me; I was scared of the unknown - scared because it took me a while to come back to my body and because this actually happened.

After all that happened, I told myself that I would never try to Astral project again. Now, after I have thought about it, I realise this is a gift and I should use it. Tell me, how I can overcome my fear of the unknown?

There is a fear of the unknown that you can overcome with experience. Fear generally can be overcome with Alchemy, which will be explained about in the Esoteric course. This gives an inner strength.

The teddy bear is likely to show you that in the state you were in; even the most harmless thing was causing you to be afraid.

Remember that negative forces use fear to stop any Astral investigation. If you give into them they will have won, but if you don't you will find a whole new world opening up for you.

Every night I practice the Fa Ra On mantra until falling asleep. I find it difficult to project with mantra. I am not used to it but I

will get used to it and practice the techniques given in these courses. I just hope it will work some day.

If you persist, you can find that it eventually works, but everything takes practice to achieve. As an alternative with the mantra Fa Ra On, pronounce it while visualising the pyramids, as realistically as you can. Look at a picture of the pyramids beforehand if you think it will help.

The physical pronouncing of the mantra aloud should not go for long, or you may not attract the sleep. When you try a mantra and you are doing it internally, do it softly so that you attract the sleep.

Week 5

Concentration

CONCENTRATION

This is a short but very important topic. Much of the success in Astral projection depends upon the ability to concentrate, and that is to focus the mind upon one thing.

If you are able to do this then Astral projection succeeds. It fails mostly due to a lack of concentration. It is the way to be able to project at will, whenever you want to, as long as there are no other factors such as illness that can stop you.

It is not easy to acquire because of the way that the mind is ordinarily used. Normally it goes on chattering throughout the day, or it is identified in whatever activity is taking place, so that one is not self-aware, which itself contributes to the chattering. Then when one goes to practise astral projection it usually fails, because the mind continues with its chattering activity.

It is the different egos, the different parts of the subconscious that bring about this chattering, but it is possible to train the mind so that it focuses on one thing. The mind can be trained, it needs to be gradually educated to be on one thing, since it is not used to operating like that.

When the mind has been trained and is focused and you practice Astral projection, the excise works very well. Using concentration I have been able to focus upon my heart, and have projected again and again, going out into the Astral and coming back, going back out again and so on.

It does take a lot of effort to acquire this ability, but if you really want to Astral project this is what you need to do. With this ability all the techniques of Astral projection work. Even the mantras require concentration to get them to work.

BEING AWARE OF WHAT YOU ARE DOING

What you need to do is to be aware of what you are doing at any moment of the day (in the way that it is written in topic 2 of this course). Wherever you are, in whatever situation, be aware of the present moment, naturally aware of the information of the five senses. Practice and investigate how it works until you get it right. Whenever you are doing an activity, concentrate upon it. Do just one thing at a time, don't do two or more activities at the same time, otherwise you will lose the focus and will easily become identified. You don't need to become mechanical or robotic to do this, practice and learn how to do it naturally.

It takes a lot of effort and willpower to do it and to maintain it throughout the day. Many sacrifices will need to be made in one way or another, but you see the results eventually, as you are more aware throughout the day and better able to concentrate on the things that you do. This also has positive effects in that you do things better and more efficiently.

Quite soon, after I discovered the importance of concentration I would go for walks, sometimes for most of the day, and would spend my whole time being aware and concentrating. This allowed me to develop this useful faculty.

With it, you are not only more aware, focussed and organised, but you are activating the spiritual part, the consciousness. It is from here that all spiritual development and progress begins. It is this part that has all the true spiritual qualities that one has; love and so on. It is with this part that you find peace. Explore and investigate the awareness, when you get it right, it will 'feel' right. It is at that moment of awareness, which is outside thought, the mind or the emotions and outside the egos, that the spiritual within is activated.

Everything takes place within the present moment. By being aware, you wake up to it.

SITTING EXERCISES

As well as this method, you can also train the mind to concentrate by using the exercises where you sit down simply to concentrate (as given in topic 2). So far, you have been practising for 10 minutes at a time. If you have been maintaining this, then increase the time to 15 minutes.

It is very important however not to force the mind. Gradually train yourself in these sitting exercises and slowly increase the time you spend doing them.

PROBLEMS WITH FALLING ASLEEP

Concentration also helps problems with falling asleep that many people who try to project experience. If you fall asleep too quickly, it helps to graduate sleep so that you are more aware going into it. If you have problems of not being able to sleep when trying to project, it is usually due to an over-active mind and a tense emotion (ego) that sometimes eventually arises. This is a consequence of a lack of concentration. Concentration attracts the sleep and stops the mind from being over-active, allowing a more successful projection.

It is possible to force the mind when trying to concentrate throughout the day. This is due to trying artificially to be aware with the mind rather than naturally activating the consciousness by practicing the awareness. You will need to investigate to learn how to be aware and concentrate on what you are doing throughout the day.

Practicing this you will find life simpler, less cluttered and less complicated, but it does require a lot of effort and sacrifice. However, if you manage to do it you will find that concentration is a very powerful tool.

USING BREAKS IN THE NIGHTS SLEEP TO INCREASE THE CHANCES OF PROJECTION

You have a greater chance of projecting into the Astral if you break your sleep and try to project many times at night. The more times you can try this the more you increase your chances of projecting. However, it is not a good idea to do this every night for long periods of time as, in the long run, the disturbed sleep will affect you adversely. So a way to do it with the least strain is to allow an extra hour of sleep when you go to bed and to set your alarm clock to wake up after your normal sleeping hours minus two or three hours. For example, if you normally sleep eight hours, set your alarm so that you wake up after five or six hours of sleep, then try the Astral again making sure that you get the remaining two or three hours sleep.

When you wake up, get up out of bed and walk around being aware, look at everything in detail; try to keep this awareness and question whether you are in the physical world or the Astral world. Keep this awareness as you go back to bed and then try your Astral exercise.

Try this exercise each week of the course from now on, at any night you choose.

In Study Centres, a practice together as a group at three in the morning has proven popular and has produced some very good results. It is not something to do frequently, but occasionally it is alright. Group exercises are especially good for getting successes, as everyone gets together and it creates a strong and positive atmosphere.

~

WEEK 5 EXERCISES

Exercise 1.

Develop your Ability to Concentrate

For this week develop your ability to concentrate with these two exercises:

1. **Practicing Awareness** - Be aware of what you are doing throughout the day, doing only one thing at a time and focussing upon whatever activity you do.

If you wish, try having a few activities where you make sure you do it, so that they become like anchors that help to maintain the daily momentum. Try being focussed upon washing, putting on your shoes and washing the dishes (or using the dishwasher if you have one).

2. **Concentration/Visualisation** - Increase the duration of your sit down concentration/visualisation exercises, putting 15 minutes as the normal standard rather than 10 as it was previously given, and increase the frequency of these exercises, so that you do two a day rather than one, for example.

This will greatly increase your ability to focus upon the technique you use for projection.

Exercise 2.

Projection to a Place

This week we are going to use the imagination and willpower to project to a place. The exercise is simple: when you go to sleep, visualise a place that you are familiar with, a park, a sacred or inspirational place you may have visited, somewhere you like to be, your house, etc.

Visualise yourself walking in it; so that it becomes concrete and real around you, as though you were walking in a real place. Imagine that you can taste, touch, feel, smell, hear and see the things in that environment in an intense and real way.

If you do this well enough you can be in that place, in that environment, once the split from the physical body takes place, and you can find yourself walking through it.

Stick to this exercise for the whole week, don't change it, this will allow you to learn more about how it works. It will be better training and you will be more able to monitor your progress throughout the week if you stick to just one technique.

Exercise 3.

Breaking the Nights Sleep

Finally, set yourself a time to wake up at night to practice projection, as described earlier in this topic.

QUESTIONS AND ANSWERS

Concentration

I have Astral travelled many times but usually it just happens with no effort. When I try to relax in bed and concentrate, I usually fall asleep. Am I doing something wrong or do I just need more practice. One more thing, my episodes of Astral travel that just happen often happen if I have stayed up much later than normal and am very tired. Thanks for any help.

It is very common to fall sleep as the exercise begins. This is because your mind needs to be trained to be on one thing. Otherwise, you fall sleep with the initial thoughts, which then become dreams immediately. You just need more practice, and as you practice the exercises more, you will learn to go further into the transition period between wakefulness and sleep. It is in that transition period that conscious Astral projection takes place. Sometimes, if you are in that transition period you think you are awake, but in fact, you could even be snoring with a very light sleep, so that you cannot even hear yourself snoring.

You get sporadic Astral experiences because you are being helped so that you learn to do it by yourself and in this way, you are taught and encouraged.

Whenever I practice the exercises, I never seem to fall asleep and, when it doesn't work, I just get up. Does this mean I am not relaxed enough or am I too aware of what is happening?

In Astral projection, it usually means that you need to develop the ability to focus the mind on one thing. If you do, you will find that you are actually able to attract sleep.

Every time I try to Astral project, it is really easy for me to relax my whole body. Then after I get the vibrations, I always seem to make it to the point of the split but then immediately my heart starts beating really fast and intensely. I always try to ignore it but it is too intense to ignore, it feels like my heart is going to blow up out of my chest! This usually stops me from making the split and

sometimes it is due to my chattering mind. I know for a fact that my heart doesn't beat like that because of any emotions like fear or nervousness because I am always very calm and concentrating hard. It is like a physical thing that comes out of nowhere. So is there any reason why this keeps happening and how do I prevent it? What is the best way to breathe to Astral project?

Try concentrating on the heart - then it doesn't matter how much it beats. Once you get used to doing it then try it with the other exercises, if there is no emotional state involved it will go back to normal.

I think I had my first Astral experience. I cannot be sure it was Astral travel. Is there a possibility of dreaming of Astral travel? The reason I ask is because in the middle of the night I sort of 'woke up,' and begun to feel the vibrations. I thought, 'OK this time I'm going to concentrate on my heart beat.' Sure enough, the vibes got deeper and more powerful and I felt I had projected (I would cast a circle before also). After flailing around in my Astral body unsure of how to use it for a few moments, I was able to get up and walk around the house. I did the conjuration of Jupiter everywhere, just in case. Then I tried to go outside my window but I was unable to. I thought, 'forget this - I'm doing it' and took a run and jumped through the wall in my living room, and ended up sort of flying outside. I tried to fly to my girlfriend's house, and I tried to fly a little way down the road - this is where my memories stop. My question: It wasn't nearly as vivid as I had been led to believe or expected it to be. Also, it happened in the middle of the night, some time after I had fallen asleep from trying the exercise. I can't be sure I was fully conscious and even during the experience it felt like I was a little out of it. Do you have tips or explanations? Also, how do I make the experience more vivid? Like daily consciousness or even more so? This would be so appreciated!

It is good to see that your efforts are paying off. It was an Astral travel experience and you did very well in your first go. Your determination, clear decision and the use of the conjurations have played a big role in it, and the fact that you were not involved in the vibrations but carried on with concentration on your heart.

The technique of the concentration on the heart normally has that effect. You can be woken up in your dreams or have a very vivid dream with very useful information for your own work; or you can be woken up in the middle of the night to try again and you took advantage of the latter.

Your experience was foggy because you need more experience. As you try more and more, you will get better at it. However, you need to get more experience in daily awareness of the moment and your level of consciousness needs to increase in the physical for your experiences in the Astral to be more vivid and clear. Some people experience a vivid Astral projection as a help, so that they know what it is like, but in your case you have been given information in the experience itself to do more than just try the technique for Astral projection. That is, you need to make efforts to do the exercises like the jump for waking up in dreams, which will help you make the experiences more vivid and more conscious.

However, ultimately, the information on the Self Knowledge course and the Esoteric course will enable you to have Astral projection experiences far beyond that which you can imagine. More importantly, you will be able to acquire esoteric knowledge that will be given to you because you got there consciously and by your own efforts.

Should we keep trying to concentrate until we eventually fall asleep? I just started the course and I have been concentrating for about 15 minutes then giving up and going to sleep on my side. I have the time to do it longer, I just never have. Also for some reason, I just cannot visualise the heart for more than 5 seconds. I can concentrate on my heartbeat, but it is a quiet beat unless I take deep breaths. Any advice welcomed thanks.

It is best to increase it gradually, if you are comfortable with 15 minutes then go onto 20 and so on. In this way, you are going to train your body and mind at concentration very well, and you are not going to be disrupted by a discomfort of any kind.

It is normal to last very little time concentrated on the heart. This is because the mind is not trained to focus on anything for long at all. You will see that as you carry on with your exercises regularly your span of concentration will increase.

Going into the details of what your heart looks like through visualising it, naturally increases the heartbeat. Try this it works very well.

Week 6

Dealing with Negative Entities

NEGATIVE ENTITIES

It is part of the structure of the way that life is created, that opposites exist; we have positive and negative, light and dark, etc.

This is necessary for life to exist; it is also necessary for learning and spiritual growth. If we had always existed in light alone, we would have no knowledge even of our own existence. It is the struggle against the darkness that makes us strong and gives us knowledge.

Therefore, we live here in this world, with all its dualities and its opposites, but these opposites also exist in the fifth dimension, that is why negative things can be experienced in dreams or in the Astral.

Just as there are divine spiritual beings, so too are there beings who are the opposite: negative beings. The beings that are divine are that way because they have created themselves to be so. The same applies for the negative beings; they have transformed themselves from humans into creatures of darkness. It is the aim of these esoteric studies to explain how to transform oneself into a being of light, for which the darkness within (the egos, the different elements of the subconscious) must be overcome and the forces of darkness outside must be defeated in their attempt to stop one from awakening. They inevitably come to try to stop anyone who takes up the spiritual work.

These beings of darkness are the ones that you may have seen in nightmares or in dreams. They are the demons that are represented in the different religions throughout the world. Many people when Astral projecting have been met by them or have sensed their presence.

They belong to a hierarchical structure of evil beings, organised according to the level of awakened evil consciousness that each of them has. There will be much more on these beings and how they are created in a future topic on the Esoteric course.

We find them in the Astral and Mental planes of the fifth dimension, although they reside in inferior dimensions (which I will explain about another time) and enter the Astral and Mental planes.

They do not as much as cause harm physically as harm someone's spiritual development. For example, when you get to the Astral there may be negative entities waiting for you there to frighten you so that you fly back to your body, or they can distract you so that you don't go somewhere more spiritual, or discover what you need to.

To the unwary, they use deceit; they can say things that are misleading and can easily fool someone into taking their advice, which inevitably is harmful for the real spiritual work. They can even appear as one's idea of holy beings, preaching about love etc, but their real purpose is to take us away from the true path.

They can stir up egos, both in the Astral and in daily life, inflaming passions and desires and leading one astray. They can cause the Astral to look unclear or darkened, they can make an initiate fall and can do works on the Astral body so that the kundalini, an essential aspect of the spiritual path, does not rise, rendering the body useless for the esoteric work.

Not long after I had begun to practice all the key elements needed to start the esoteric path, I was giving lectures in a city when two new students joined. They looked like two angels, young and with blonde hair, and impressed me with their ability to Astral project at will every night.

The woman had been in the national newspapers as many people had supposedly seen her flying over the top of a building. I was impressed, but I began to have doubts. The way they had achieved their powers was not through the slow hard work that each of us must do, but had supposedly started after a car crash in which they should have died.

Doubts appeared too, when we left them in a room with a pentagram. The pentagram is a symbol that protects against evil forces when it is used the right way up (more on this in the future). After they left the room, I noticed that the pentagram had been taken down and was placed the wrong way up.

One night in the Astral, I saw the person doing a work on my spine, where the kundalini rises, and inserting things into my kidneys that blocked the flow of energy. After this, a master of the White Lodge called Rabolu appeared to me in the Astral and gave me a Century plant (again, more on this in the future), which is used for protection. Then I asked the beings of light to undo what the negative beings had done to me. I conducted an exercise with a group of people (one that will be explained in a future course) to break their evil influence. I saw them both the next day and they looked completely different. Gone was the angelic look, instead they looked like a couple of vampires, their faces were even swollen and they were only able to babble a load of rubbish.

We never saw them physically after that, although some months later I met the person again in the Astral. This time however, I commanded him to reveal himself to me. He lifted into the air, turned into a grotesque demon and disappeared into the darkness from where he came.

These were two people who had awakened their consciousness for evil, but this time thanks to the protection of the beings of light, they had failed in their evil mission.

This example is very unusual, because such beings are mostly found when we go to the Astral. Some of you on the course have already experienced a little of these negative entities from experiences in the Astral, and those of you who will go there in the future are very likely to meet them, even more so if you actually take up the spiritual work properly.

There are many cases in history and folklore of these beings. One very well recorded type of encounter happens when a person is partly in the Astral, lying in bed and feels totally paralysed, sensing or seeing a negative entity close by or actually in contact with them. These entities can take advantage of that natural time when we are not quite in the physical body and not quite detached in the Astral and so are unable to move.

In times like this, you can use what we call conjurations, which are words that dispel evil entities.

CONJURATIONS

These are phrases that have the power to return negative entities back to their abode or to disable them. They have been used throughout history and references can be found in many esoteric texts. They work best when done strongly with a lot of conviction and when one's energies are strong.

Whenever you see an evil entity in the Astral, or a being that you are unsure of, or if you go into the Astral and its dark, or in the physical world if you sense a negative vibe or presence, or before going to sleep, you should use them.

There are two that you can use: 'Jupiter' and 'Bellilin'. They are both available as sound files (see page 94).

Jupiter

To do this conjuration, you place your left hand over your solar plexus, which is around the navel. This protects against evil entities while the conjuration is being pronounced.

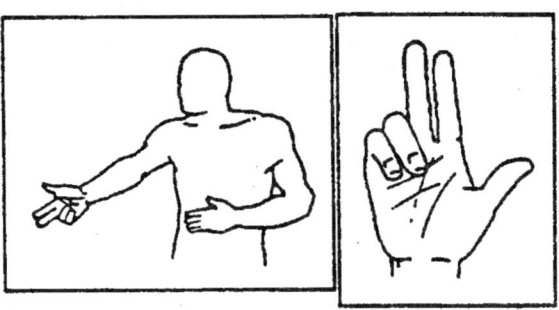

Put your fingers of your right hand in the shape of a gun with the index and middle fingers extended, the other two fingers closed and the thumb up. You extend your arm straight in front of you, pointing at the entity if you see one, and then pronounce the following words three times:

> *In the name of Jupiter,*
> *Father of Gods,*
> *I conjure you,*
> *Te Vigos Cosilim.*

Say that over three times.

If you are in the Astral you can sometimes see rays coming out of your hand, so you can imagine the rays as you do it in the physical world.

Bellilin

You don't need to do anything with your arms with this one; you sing it, using the sound file as a guide to learn it.

Here are the words - you pronounce it three times:

> *Bellilin, Bellilin, Bellilin,*
> *Amphora of salvation,*
> *I would like to be next to you,*
> *Materialism has no strength next to me,*
> *Bellilin, Bellilin, Bellilin.*

This conjuration is particularly useful if for some reason you cannot move or cannot put your hands into position for the conjuration of Jupiter.

You can access the sound files for these conjurations by typing the following addresses in your Internet browser:
http://www.gnosticweb.org/astralbook/Jupiter.mp3
http://www.gnosticweb.org/astralbook/Bellilin.mp3

You need to say both conjurations all the way through three times for them to be fully effective.

There is no need to be frightened if the entity is still there while you are still pronouncing the conjuration, although it can sometimes disappear once you begin the conjuration. If it is there while you are doing it, continue and the conjuration will be effective as soon as you finish.

I remember a horrible animal attacking me in the Astral. As soon as I saw it, I began to use Jupiter, because it is faster. It started running at me and bit me on the arm, even though I was conjuring it. I continued to conjure and the animal stayed there. It only left when I had completed the conjuration totally.

If for any reason you come across something and you are not sure whether it is from the good side or from the evil side - use a conjuration to check. If it's good it will stay, if it's bad, it will usually go, or be disabled.

Many people have been deceived by these entities, so if in doubt, conjure. Also, use your intuition, because sometimes you can tell an evil entity just by looking at it, particularly if you look into its eyes, they can look dark and evil. Many times, I have been met by an entity who took the form of a spiritual guide in order to deceive me, but you can learn to tell just by looking into their eyes what they really are. If you see that they are evil, conjure them.

In the Astral, you can call spiritual beings and get help and teachings from them. However, often if you call, a negative entity will arrive that looks exactly like the spiritual being you are calling, so use your intuition and conjure if you need to. If the entity is evil it will go, if it is the real one, it will stay, and don't worry; the good ones don't get offended if you conjure them.

You can also use the conjurations at night before you go to sleep, so that you clear away any negative entities that may be there or may appear during the night.

In this case, if you have made sure that your room is clear, you will then need to seal yourself or your room so that nothing can get back in. You do this by drawing a circle of protection around you.

Circle of Protection
This forms a barrier that stops any evil entity from entering. It is drawn in a circle, using the imagination and doing a work with the elementals of nature, which makes the circle strong and sustains it.

Elementals of nature are essences of creatures that are evolving. They have been known throughout history in various myths and legends, as for example, fairies, pixies, gnomes, salamanders, sylphs, etc.

They have been used by ancient peoples to protect sacred or important things. We hear tales, for example, of ancient burial grounds being protected by loads of snakes, or by swarms of bees.

Overlooking the town where I grew up was an ancient burial site. Legends said that these sites were protected by bees and indeed, there were very many recorded cases of people disrupting the sites and being attacked by bees. When some unemployed people were made to work for their unemployment benefit by cutting steps into the burial site, they were chased away by swarms of bees that seemed to appear out of nowhere.

Many ancient peoples knew how to work with these elementals of nature; they are the same ones that we use for this circle.

Having conjured away, then you draw the circle as follows:

> Say these words:
> *My Father please, order my elemental intercessor to wrap a magical circle of protection around me (or the bed or the room, whatever), so that no evil entity can harm me.*

The Father is the male aspect of each one's own Being. We ask that part of our Being, because he has the power to do it.

Then you imagine a circle, formed by a beam of light, being drawn around wherever you have chosen.

You do this three times making sure that the circle is joined and complete.

This can be done before going to bed at night, or at any time that you feel you need to do it. Then once it's done, no evil entity can get in. The circle stays until you move out of it; when you move out of it, you break it.

A student of ours once was a bit sceptical, but nevertheless he drew the circle around him before going to sleep. He woke up in the Astral to find himself unable to move, with an evil looking cat in front of him. He became frightened and started spitting at the cat, because that was all he thought he could do. Then he noticed that he had a circle of light around him and that the cat could not get in. He then woke up, back in his body. He should have practiced the conjuration of Bellilin more because he could have used it to make the cat disappear.

Jesus used this circle of protection when he protected a woman who was about to be stoned. He drew a circle in the sand around her and she was saved.

The more that you practice these conjurations, the more you will remember to use them and remember the words to them in the Astral. You can also find yourself using them in your dreams if you practice them enough.

Once you actually use them, you see just how effective they are and you realise that you are able to deal with negative entities and to go and get teachings in the Astral, unhindered by them.

So practice them and get them right, because you will need them.

～

WEEK 6 EXERCISES

Exercise 1.

Use the Conjurations and the circle of protection - Practice them as written above, enough times so that they are recorded in your subconscious and you do them in your dreams or in the Astral.

Exercise 2.

To Astral Project - Continue with the technique to project using mantras. You still need to be able to concentrate upon the mantra and, in order to go back to visualisation techniques (as we will soon do in future topics) you will need to have maintained your ability to concentrate upon what you are doing and to visualise. Therefore, we are going to continue with what is important to maintain and increase these while we use mantras.

These weekly exercises are most important for getting into the Astral. If you do them all methodically each day this week you will have a much better chance of being able to succeed than if you just try a mix of things here and there.

1. **Mantras** – Try two different ones this week. Develop each one properly and - learn about how each one works. They are all slightly different and each different sound has a different effect on the chakras, so if you keep to a particular one for long enough you will activate that chakra much more, making the exercise more effective.

2. **Visualising an object for ten minutes each day** – Vary the objects, for example, a glass of water, a plant, flowers, etc and continue with at least ten minutes each day. Remember to close your eyes when you are recreating the object in your mind and to recreate it often.

Don't try to stay there with your eyes open or force yourself to keep staring at the object for a long period of time. Begin with just a little and gradually increase the time you spend on this exercise.

Exercise 3.

To wake up in dreams

   1. **Questioning where you are** - Ask whether you are in the physical world or in the Astral world by using the jump and pulling your finger and by seeing if there is anything strange around you, in the ways that I have described above. Remember to genuinely question, looking around you with as much awareness as you can and try it as often as you can.

   2. **Practicing Awareness** - Being aware during the day. Help this exercise to work by making sure you try when you do the three things I mentioned last week –whenever you are washing yourself, putting your shoes on and eating.

   3. **Practicing Awareness and Questioning** – Go for a walk for 10-15 minutes each day and intensively practice being aware and practicing questioning which dimension you are in by pulling the finger and jumping.

Exercise 4.

To Remember Dreams - Lying still when you wake up, going back over the night's dreams and using the mantra Raom Gaom.

~

QUESTIONS AND ANSWERS

Q. What does Amphora mean? Does it have a translation? Does it mean jug or container?

A. Yes, Amphora means a container, but one of a spiritual nature.

What does 'Te Vigos Cosilim' Mean? Who is Bellilin? What does it mean?

They are both words that dispel evil that come from the higher dimensions. They do not have a literal translation here, although the Hindus used Bellilin representing a wind that casts away evil.

Are there also other ways of dealing with negative entities besides the conjurations and circle? I have heard that if you mention Jesus' name these entities disappear.

Pronouncing a master's name is not a reliable way of getting rid of them. You will find it more effective to use one of these conjurations on the course rather than using the name of a master. In any case, negative entities often appear in disguise when you invoke a master in the Astral.

Do we create some of these entities from negative habits like negative thinking or even smoking?

These entities are beings that have awakened in evil; however there are entities that are created by people, called larvae. These predominate in places where there is a lot of emotion, for example in a room where there has been a lot of anger or drunkenness. These larvae harm the Astral body.

There are also ones that are created by sexual desires and these are called incubus or succubus. They have an existence outside of the individual and they have to be destroyed with an alchemical work, which is explained in the Esoteric course.

There are also the parts of the subconscious that affect the Astral, which we call egos; these are various elements such as anger, pride, fear, etc. These will be explained about in detail in the Self Knowledge course.

When you dream about a negative creature does that mean that in the Astral there is a negative entity that is working on you? I had a dream about a Vampire Bat and it flew down and bit me on the left shoulder. It felt so real and I couldn't get it off of me. I woke up and my shoulder felt funny. So was something harming me in the Astral and I just didn't realise I was in the Astral?

Yes it can be, they do attack at night like that and bats in the Astral can also have associations with black magic. However animals attacking can also symbolise egos that are attacking.

While drawing the circle of protection do I also have to say the statement three times, or is only the circle to be drawn three times?

You have to say the statement three times and draw the circle three times as well.

I understand that negative entities not only affect us in the Astral but in the physical plane also. Can we use the conjurations and circle of protection in the physical plane also to keep negative entities away?

Yes, you can also use the conjurations and circle of protection in the physical plane to keep negative entities away if you feel you need to.

Will the circle of protection keep negative entities away from me only or all the persons that are within the circle of protection?

The circle can protect everyone inside it as long as no one goes in or out of it and breaks it.

Can I create a circle of protection around others, even if I am not in the circle? If yes in that case what will be the statement?

Yes you can draw it around others even if you are not in it. You say everything the same as when you draw it around yourself except that instead of asking it to be drawn around yourself, you ask for it to be drawn around the people.

Since my Lord is Christ (not the lesser god, Jupiter), how am I going to protect myself when I Astral travel? I cannot invoke Jupiter for protection because I don't believe lesser Gods. Can I invoke Christ for protection instead?

Jupiter is another name for the 'Father' and he is very important in Christianity. These are just names for the same thing; it's not worth getting stuck over them. If you stick to the rigid confines of a religion you will not be able to progress esoterically. If you want to be an esotericist you have to ask yourself what you really know and whether you only want to believe, because experience is needed to discover the truth. If you try this conjuration you will see that it works.

As I lay in bed, right before the Astral split, in the moment of paralysis a form descended on me in my bed. I fought out of fear at first and tried to fight it off, but I felt nothing there. Then finally I felt an arm wrap around me and I touched it with my Astral body. It was not threatening, but benign and unthreatening. Last night as I lay upon the couch and drifted off, at the moment of the split, and the paralysis, I felt an animal that seemed like a cat, jump upon the couch and lie upon me. I tried out of fear to smack it away but nothing was there, only making myself move to regain bodily control. This repeated over and over until I let the fear go, and then I could feel it. I was feeling it with my Astral arms not the physical ones. The first step is in learning how our Astral body is different from our physical, and we don't move them in the same way. I am learning, all be it small steps, but the most amazing thing about it is, someone is helping me, showing me things. I am slowly but surely going down a new road, and am growing into much more than I was before.

There are negative entities that use that very common Astral experience known as sleep paralysis to frighten people and put them off the Astral and esoteric things. They sometimes take the shape of animals. It is likely that this is what you are seeing, not the spiritual being that is helping you. To check this, use the conjuration all the way through and see what happens to the entity.

Since this lecture, every night before I hit the pillow, I have conjured the house and asked for a circle of protection around the entire house. Although I have not knowingly experienced anything that would indicate I needed to protect my house in this manner before now, I try to be diligent and practice what I'm learning.
After forgetting to conjure and circle one night, everything you said came true and I have no hesitation in heeding every word of advice offered on this subject!
As I said, I have never knowingly been troubled by negative entities before, but it seems that now they know what I'm up to, they really are out to annoy me!

Yes, they really are there. There is a huge war going on between the forces of light and darkness, most of this is unknown to the average person.

Having the right tools is enabling me to observe aspects of fear and have the potential to deal effectively with each issue that arises. I agree that ultimately there isn't actually anything to fear, it's just a matter of proving it to myself, which gives me solid confidence.

In your experience, is an individual's level of spiritual development likely to be tested to the same degree by negative entities?

The more we progress spiritually, the more the negative entities attack us and try to stop us. They see us then as people who are getting away from their grip and who begin to pose a threat to them.

The further into the light we go the more the darkness comes against us.

I am glad to get these tools. I have had several friends who have become very involved in the psychic without really having any interest in the spiritual work that must go along with it. Without an exception, they have all been negatively influenced by it within a couple of years. I was interested in such things at first myself, but was always more interested in self-awareness and knowledge than in the psychic and other 'parlor games'.

I had a situation a couple of years ago with a friend who had developed her clairvoyant skill fairly highly, and had put together an informal class dealing with different topics. I didn't take it too seriously and out of curiosity decided to attend. I had been working with awareness and self-knowledge, but didn't take seriously the need to protect myself. One night I attended her class, but in the early hours of the morning I was awakened with a strange sensation. It is very difficult to explain the sensation, but similar to an extreme shame or ego attack.

Now, I am not prone to huge bouts of shame or anxiety, but not knowing what was going on, didn't halt it soon enough. After a while, I realised it was an attack, and I was able to stop it immediately. Although not soon enough, and by the time I woke

up, I was physically sick. I literally felt de-energized for months. It taught me a very valuable lesson/s though. Don't set yourself up for these attacks. Protect yourself. Practice awareness: don't be where (if you can help it) these influences are being called upon. I would not go around to this woman, or classes such as that, for anything

You are quite right about those entities and about dealing with them and avoiding harmful places.
Self Knowledge is a vital basis for development, because the esoteric path is all about inner transformation.

I was just wondering whether these are things that must be said aloud, or may be said silently in the mind.

You say them aloud, because the word has strength and because then you do it aloud in a dream or in the Astral too and it has more power there.
It depends on the situation in the physical though, because there are times when you have to pronounce it silently.

At one stage I remember rising slowly towards the ceiling from my bed. Then all of a sudden, I heard a very evil growl right beside me. It was what I thought at the time my cat. However, my cat is only a kitten and I remember thinking this can't be my kitten making such a noise. Anyway, I remember this growl was stopping me to fully project and then it was simply over. Does this sound like a negative entity? I didn't really feel scared at the time because I thought to myself that this is not real and I said for it to go away. Then I felt it was quite over-powering and I didn't succeed to project.

Yes, it was a negative entity. If you had used Belillin then it would have gone away. As it was, it succeeded in its attempt to stop you in the Astral. Next time you will have learned from this and will be able to get rid of anything negative that appears.

When the two (angelic) people turned up to the course, and showed special powers, were these powers seen in the physical? How did they obtain these powers? (i.e. Were they tricked by

other negative entities, was there a transfer of energy?)
Do these powers manifest in all of us already (positive and negative)?
What would have happened to them if they had resorted to doing good rather than evil?
Would they have still disappeared in the physical after doing well, and re-joined the Wheel, or remained in the Astral off the Wheel?

No, these powers were seen in the Astral at the time, but there were reports in the local newspaper by people who had seen the woman hovering in the air in the physical. The dark side always likes to show off powers.

They consciously awakened in evil, just as some of us here are working to awaken in light.

No these powers have to be developed, although the forces of light and darkness exist within everyone.

They would have had to repent and want to change, and then they would have had to start the esoteric work from the beginning like everyone else.

They would start in the physical like anyone else and stay on the Wheel unless they eventually managed to progress far enough to get off.

If you use the circle of protection and the conjurations around newborn babies, is this beneficial in saving them from the harm of negative entities and their egos from previous lives?

Yes, it can be beneficial to protect them from outside evil entities, although they are much less susceptible to attacks than adults, because fewer of their egos have manifested and their essence manifests more.

Is there any shield of protection that moves with you, without breaking to protect you from sinister beings?

There is a work with an elemental of a Century plant, which gives a more all-round protection; this is given in a later course.

Last night I resumed working on trying to Astral travel in accordance with this weeks assigned practices and I have had some

success! I began by doing the conjuration and drawing the magical circle and then recited the mantra FaRaOn, which I haven't tried before.

I must have gone straight to sleep but after about an hour I found that I was awake in the middle of a dream and began walking around and doing things as though I was awake! While walking around I found that I was able to walk through things. It was then that a bad entity attacked me. I was grabbed from behind - I turned around and saw that it was non-human, possibly an ego as I think I have seen it before. So I applied the Jupiter conjuration and it worked! After saying it three times the entity disappeared. Then I did some flying.

I still haven't been able to Astral travel straight away by rising out of the body but continue to work on it. I have succeeded in remembering and using the conjurations so I am feeling pleased.

You see, if you practice the techniques given here they do work.

I think it may help me to know more about the negative entities. Do we find out more about the Lodge's etc?

There will be more information on negative entities in future courses. They are fallen beings who are awakened in darkness.

I have had experiences where I was threatened by beings. In these experiences I seem to be conscious that I am dreaming in the Astral when I am threatened. I still feel unclear as to when it is an experience in the Astral, or whether it is my subconscious producing these experiences. Is there a way to tell?

You get to know whether something is real or whether it is a projection from the subconscious through experience, by using your intuition and with progress in the elimination of the egos (the elements of the subconscious).

In either case, you should use the conjurations if you see any negative entities and are aware enough to, then you will get rid of them.

I had a strange experience last night, while asleep. I woke up suddenly after a vision of a rock band in black. One of the people from it I recognised from the past. I woke up feeling I was being

shown negative beings. It felt like it was connected to my questioning at the moment regarding negative entities. I still find it difficult to differentiate whether it has come from my own subconscious or from the Astral. Should I be going with the initial feelings when I wake up? I have found several times in this course I have my questions answered in dreams. Is this a reliable source? Is it common?

Yes, go with the initial feeling you had when you woke up. Information is given through dreams so you need to be able to differentiate between those and projections from the subconscious.

Answers to problems are quite common in dreams, that are the place where we get direct teachings. Things do get clearer though with the elimination of the egos and the whole esoteric work in general.

Can you really be sure of the nature of bodhisattvas? I would like to share my story. My brother's son had what was said to be an imaginary friend. I discovered in that month that it was not imaginary.

As I slept one evening, I was awakened to the sensation of a child-sized figure jumping up and down on me. When I began to awaken, it ran away giggling; yet there was no one physically there in my room with me. A couple of nights later, my father experienced the same encounter, and testified to it without first hearing of my own encounter. My father was a total skeptic of all things paranormal. This spirit paid visits to me for over a year, and after a time, the sleep disruptions became irritating and I was no longer a willing participant in the games. The spirit came to me again, this time appearing in a strange, cherubic form. It said, "I don't want to be dead anymore. You need to open up so I can get in." I began to realise that this spirit was no innocent little boy. It was evil, if not a full-fledged demon.

My point is that these bodhisattvas may not be what they appear.

You are confusing a negative entity with a bodhisattva as what you saw was a negative entity. As you have experienced, there are many negative entities wishing to deceive anyone who is searching for knowledge. That's why it's important to learn to use the conjurations to check whether something is good or bad and to know what the esoteric path is.

A true bodhisattva is a person in the physical world who has incarnated their Master or Spirit. If someone has this (they are extremely rare) you can invoke their Master or Being who is part of them and who looks like them and he will appear. If in doubt, you should use the conjurations to check whether the Being is good or evil, if it is evil, it will go or become disabled, so you invoke the Master again until the spiritual one appears. You can only do this with people (bodhisattvas) who have their Master incarnated and the Master has its own name, the immortal name.

Week 7

Astral and Dream Experiences

In this topic we are going to look into what happens in dreams and in the Astral, how you can understand the things you see and experience there and the kind of things that you can best do while you are consciously in the Astral plane.

The language of the Astral is intuitive and symbolic so, to understand it you need to develop and use your intuition, to gain experience of being there and to progress along the esoteric path thereby awakening psychic faculties and consciousness.

You can also get a basic understanding to start with by reading the information given on these courses, particularly the Esoteric course. By the time you complete that you should have a wider understanding of the esoteric work, because in the Astral basically everything relates to that.

USING INTUITION

It is most important to use intuition when interpreting the meaning of a dream or an Astral experience because of the intuitive and symbolic nature of the language of the Astral. Each symbol there can have many different meanings. Each is relevant to the one who experiences them even though there are symbols with universal meanings.

Intuition is a sense that allows us to capture information from a higher plane that could not otherwise be gained from the mind or from the five senses. The information reaches us from a spiritual part within that is located in the higher dimensions. It is one of several psychic faculties that can be developed on these courses and can be very useful to have.

Intuition works immediately. When you remember a dream, you get a first feeling about what things mean. Go with that feeling without allowing the mind to come in and reason, because the ordinary mind lacks that higher connection.

We can be forewarned of danger and other things because events that are going to happen often take place in the higher dimensions first and information from those dimensions can reach us here.

Everyone carries this sense to a certain extent and probably most have experienced it. The problem however, is that most people do not develop it or pay attention to it. The Self Knowledge course explains how to activate it while the Esoteric course explains how to develop and awaken it and other faculties. Everyone has it, so begin to use it when you want to discover the meaning of a dream or Astral experience.

SYMBOLS IN THE ASTRAL

Much of what is seen in dreams in the beginning of the work are the projections of the subconscious, so intuition should be used to tell where they are coming from. It is very important to learn about the subconscious and how the psyche works, because you can then take the steps to clear the elements of the subconscious, which we call 'egos'.

Without this, Astral experiences are always subject to the subjective projections of the subconscious.

Generally, dreams and Astral experiences have a symbolic side. If you look at a dream plainly there may be nothing much to it, but when you recall your first intuitive feeling about it when you wake up, you know that it is referring to a certain aspect of your life. It is giving information about a person, a situation, etc. and you know what it is and what is going to happen. In this way, you gradually begin to interpret your dreams and experiences and the symbols in them. It is very useful for inner development, because as you gradually remember your dreams more and more you intuitively know that a particular dream is telling you what aspect in your life you must change, what egos you urgently need to work upon, which situations are harming you, or are harming others, etc.

In the Astral, a particular symbol may sometimes have different meanings and the right one can be grasped through intuition. It is important though not to tell any esoteric symbols that you may see in the Astral to anyone, because secrecy is very important there and if you tell others, whoever they are, you may not be shown any more for some time.

WHAT TO DO IN THE ASTRAL

It is very easy to waste an opportunity to learn something important when you go to the Astral; time spent flying around nowhere in particular, looking at details on walls, etc. it is not the best way to use an Astral experience. It is better to get esoteric experiences.

Sometimes these experiences are given anyway and are there when you Astral travel, for example you may wake up in the Astral in a situation that is full of symbolic meanings for you. At other times however, you have to seek out the learning.

This can be done by asking your divine Being (either the divine Mother or Father, who are the male and female aspects of the Being) to take you where you need to go, then they can take you somewhere.

Alternatively, you can go to a temple to be taught. If you know one, concentrate upon it or ask your divine Being to take you to the Gnostic Temple to be taught. Don't be surprised if you are not allowed in, because often a certain level of esoteric work is needed to get into many of them.

Another option is to invoke a master. These are spiritual beings who are awake in the higher dimensions. Everyone has their own master, which is incarnated within a person if they progress enough along the esoteric path. Then the person gets the title 'Master', but it is the part of the Being that is really a master. You may know of some already and can invoke them, but be warned, because some that you have read about could now have fallen and be a demon, since they can rise and fall (there will be more explained about this on the esoteric course). At other times, a negative entity can appear first, so you need to use the conjurations if you are in any doubt. Also, people can call themselves masters here in the physical world but they have not incarnated their being and therefore do not have the true esoteric title of 'Master', so calling them in the Astral is a waste of time and can easily lead to being deceived.

TRAVELLING

There are different ways to travel somewhere in the Astral and using your intuition at the time is a good guide. You can always walk in the Astral but it is much quicker to fly. You can be taken somewhere if you ask, or you can concentrate upon a specific place and you can go there immediately. Alternatively, travel from the spot you are in using what you see there to guide you. If you want to go back to a place, you have been to before, visualise it and you can go there.

It is possible to concentrate upon a place and project there directly, as the exercise in this topic explains. Or as you go to sleep, you may see dream images. Concentrate upon one of them and go into it, and then you can go directly into it and be in the Astral.

If you are already in a place in which you are being taught, stay there and continue the learning unless it is time to go.

Don't worry about being stuck in the Astral, we always come back unless the physical body dies. You just wake up from sleep, or more often straight away after the experience. The difficulty is staying in the Astral without going back to the body. It helps to hold onto something that is Astral, to stay aware to avoid the experience from becoming a dream and to watch the emotions, since any emotion can bring you back quickly. Emotions such as fear and worry are major culprits.

If you get there and can't see, conjure away; an ego or a negative entity could be the problem.

Sometimes in the Astral, a being can appear in front of you, sometimes telling you different things. Through intuition, you can tell if that being is good or evil just by looking at them and using that sense. If you look into their eyes, you can often tell what they are, because the eyes can uncover the evil ones.

Through the process of the esoteric path, the consciousness is gradually awakened. That means that you clear the consciousness of those elements (egos) that make up the subconscious. Then in daily life, you are more aware and are more aware in dreams until the consciousness is awakened.

The level of teachings that someone gets is entirely due to their capacity to understand and receive them. This is according to the level of spiritual development that one has, which you can learn to progress in on the Self Knowledge and Esoteric courses.

The real way to get profound wisdom and understanding is to

take up the esoteric path. The capacity for wisdom contained in the ordinary consciousness is very limited. The knowledge about oneself and life that is attainable is small for an ordinary person compared with what it is possible to achieve on the path.

On the path, spiritual beings both in the Astral and in their influence upon events of everyday life, put events and situations so that the person can be tested, situations that test how the person acts in relation to anger, or honesty for instance. By doing this the spiritual beings can see how prepared someone is to receive true knowledge. It is not just given to anyone because then it is not valued and is easily rubbished and abused.

Knowledge is given according to ones own merits, when someone is prepared for it and has earned it. It is given according to the capacity and level of spiritual development of the person.

∼

WEEK 7 EXERCISES

This week there is a different technique to Astral project using visualisation, so have a go at this for this week. The concentration that you have been (hopefully) building up with your 10-15 minute concentration/visualisation exercises will be put to good use here.

The exercises in the weeks following will be about getting into the Astral and on the Esoteric course; they will be about getting teachings in the Astral.

Note that these weekly exercises are most important for getting into the Astral. If you do them all methodically each day this week you will have a much better chance of being able to succeed than if you just try a mix of things here and there.

Exercise 1.

To Astral Project: Projection to a Room
This week you are going to try to project into a room in the house

where you live. Before you go to sleep, go into the room that you intend to project into and study it in great detail. Walk around and use all of your senses to perceive it. Take as long as you need to really take everything in and to feel present and aware in the place. If another person lives in the house with you who know about the Astral, ask him or her to place an object in the room, an object that you know, but it should be put in a place that you do not know. Remember to study the object as well before you go to sleep.

Then go to sleep visualising the room in great detail, placing yourself back in it with your imagination, with the intention of projecting there and discovering where the object was placed. If you don't have any one in the house who can place an object, then visualise just the room and try to project there.

If you do this, well enough you can rise out of your body or go to that place once the split from the physical body takes place.

Of course, you don't need to stay in the room for the whole time that you are in the Astral; you can leave your room and travel.

Don't forget to use the conjurations and circle of protection before you go to sleep.

Exercise 2.

Practice the exercises from previous weeks

    1.   To Prepare to Astral Project - the following will make Astral projection more effective:

- To concentrate the mind on activities in daily life.

- To practice concentration/visualisation for ten or more minutes once or twice each day.

Much of the failure in Astral projection comes because the mind is not trained to be on one thing. It is used to chattering away all day, then when you try to do an exercise to project, the mind carries on chattering, so it is important to train it, increasing the ability to focus it on what you need to.

a)   To concentrate the mind on activities in daily life - This tackles the way the mind is used. Normally it just runs of its own accord, resulting in an almost continuous state of daydreaming. It can however be trained so that it becomes an effective tool, which can be used as is needed.

The important thing is to concentrate upon whatever activity you are doing at the time and to do only one activity at a time. Even if you have many tasks to do and are under pressure, deal with the most important one, giving it your full attention, even if it is just for a few moments before you have to do another task. Give whatever you are doing at that moment your full attention.

This needs to be done throughout the day. To help to get to that, concentrate upon three activities that you do each day, making the effort to use them to practice being concentrated upon what you are doing.

Any activity can be used, but try these three, whatever way other things are going during the day, use them to anchor yourself in concentration:

- Washing yourself.

- Putting your shoes on and taking them off.

- Washing the dishes.

Concentrate upon each of these activities, not allowing the mind to interfere. If you have thoughts go straight back to the activity you are doing, investigate how concentration works, then apply it throughout the day.

b) Visualising an object for ten minutes each day – Take an object, it can be any object. Sit down and place it where you can see it clearly. Then, concentrate upon it in great detail, observing how it looks, textures, shapes, colours, the way that light reflects on it, etc, everything you can about it. When you have clearly seen it, then close your eyes and recreate the object exactly as it is in your mind. If there are things that you cannot recreate because you did not look at them properly, or if the image is fading away, open your eyes and look at it again, study it, then close your eyes and recreate the image again in your mind. Keep doing this process so that you visualise it as clearly as you can. Do this for 10 minutes each day, then continue with your exercise of Astral projection at night. If you want to do this for more times each day then do it, but increase it very gradually, because the mind needs to be educated and you should not force it.

Vary the objects, for example, a glass of water, a plant, flowers, etc. and continue with at least ten minutes each day. Remember to close your eyes when you are recreating the object in your mind and to recreate it often.

Don't try to stay there with your eyes open or force yourself to keep staring at the object for a long period of time. Gradually increase the time you spend on this exercise. Begin with jut a little.

2. To wake up in dreams

a) Questioning where you are - Ask whether you are in the physical world or in the Astral world by using the jump and pulling your finger and by seeing if there is anything strange around you, in the ways that I have described. Remember to genuinely question, looking around you with as much awareness as you can and try it as often as you can.

b) Practicing Awareness - Being aware during the day. Help this exercise to work by making sure you try when you do the three things I mentioned above –whenever you are washing yourself, putting your shoes on and eating.

c) Practicing Awareness and Questioning – Go for a walk for 10-15 minutes each day and intensively practice being aware and questioning which dimension you are in by pulling the finger and jumping.

3. To remember dreams

Lie still when you wake up and go back over the night's dreams. Use the mantra Raom Gaom.

~

QUESTIONS AND ANSWERS

Q. I just wanted to know if there are any rules that we should follow when in the Astral. I don't want to get there and do something that will offend anyone or anything! Also if you went to the Astral and saw something like a building that only existed in the Astral, and you described it to me and then I went to look at it, would I see the same thing as you or is the building represented to us based on our own individual experiences and thoughts (if that is how things work at all in the Astral)?

A. The more you know about the esoteric work the better, because the symbols relate to it. However, you can still use your commonsense and intuition, remembering that you are there primarily to receive spiritual information. Of course, don't do anything sexual or go along with any evil entities.

Things can sometimes be there because they do exist in the Astral and others can see them. Many things that exist there do not exist here. Things can also be put there for a teaching, or can be projections of the mind. Again, you can use your intuition and gain experience, because experience makes things gradually clearer.

On a recent Astral experience, I was taken somewhere and I was shown some things I did not understand at the time. The first was of what appeared to be an ancient wall. On this wall were round objects that upon closer observation became scenes of different people and different times. The only thing that comes to mind is the Wheel of Samsara. Was this an esoteric symbol, to teach me?

Yes this very much sounds like symbols that were used in the Astral to teach you. If you don't understand them now, remember them very well. If you continue this work and your capacity and consciousness increases, along with the information that you get from this course, you will find that you can understand the things that seemed to be obscure in the beginning.

Does the "infinity symbol" have any significance? Likewise, does classical music have any significance?

The "infinity symbol" has a meaning; it is a true esoteric symbol.

It represents the cycles of evolution and involution, which travel round and round, represented by the figure eight, from existence to existence. The real spiritual work is needed to get off this cycle. The symbol can be found in the ninth sphere, which means that the work with Alchemy needs to be carried out. Classical music can be spiritual; there is music in the higher dimensions, which is very significant to certain experiences. The symbol of infinity is an esoteric symbol, so you shouldn't say anything about these kind of things to anyone if you see them in the Astral, they are given to the individual and if they are spoken about; darkness follows and you may not be shown things. In the esoteric world, the ability to be silent is important

When you say not to mention anything about these symbols - does that include to you in these questions and answers or just in my "everyday life"?
I have had no real new experience since this one - is this because I spoke about it (also I have been quite sick and run down with a bad toothache - hopefully this is the reason)? Because of the above, I didn't do my exercises for about a week – I see what you mean about loosing what you built up very quick.

It includes everyone, but distinguishes between ordinary experiences and the truly esoteric ones.
Both speaking about personal esoteric information and illness can bring about the loss of experiences. When the continuity in the exercises is lost, it needs to be built up again. Don't force the body to practice when you are ill though.

A comment of yours in your lecture on dreams struck me as being strange at the time. You said that it might be useful to keep a diary of your dreams but to keep it secret. If I see symbols in the future and keep a record of them, is this OK as long as I keep it secret?

Yes, you should not have any problems with writing things in the diary as long as you keep them secret.

The other night was the first time I have ever consciously got up in the Astral. I made the conscious decision to gently roll out of bed. I was not even sure it worked but then it was as if the lights

came on and I was somewhere else. I took that little jump and floated along effortlessly through walls and any object. I went through a plate glass window and hovered above the trees, I did not know where to go since I did not know where I was. This confusion brought me back to the comfort of my bed. I went back in the Astral several more times, as I often do, but when I tried to pass through a different wall, I thudded to the floor. Is this common? What was holding me back the next few times; it was as if the walls were solid!

The problem with the wall was your mind. Doubts cause that problem. Push into the wall with your hand so that it starts to go through, then follow through with the rest of your body.

I've heard that you should be careful when shape shifting in the Astral because you could come back with a part of that animal and start developing some of its wild characteristics. I would really appreciate your comments on this. Is there danger there?

No you can't come back as an animal by doing that, what you are doing has nothing to do with the process of birth and death. You would do best to forget about shape shifting because it is a projection of the mind. Go into the Astral clear of that and get some real spiritual teachings.

Week 7

First Supplementary Topic
General Dream Symbols

GENERAL DREAM SYMBOLS

Here is a guide to the meaning of some symbols that are given in the Astral and dreams; the starting point for it was found in the work of Samael Aun Weor who gave many symbols in his books. You can use it as a general guide only, because there are other meanings to many of the symbols. Much depends upon the particular circumstances of the experiences too and using your own intuition is vital.

Also bear in mind that objects that you see may or may not have a symbolic meaning. Many things may be representations of the mind and may have no value. Again your intuition will guide you if you have practiced enough and can use it.

There are not many questions and answers related to symbols, because they are for the dreamer to discover their meaning. Also because I don't want to spend my time as a dream guide. It is better for me to explain how to walk along the path, to give the tools to do so and for me to teach you how to learn to understand the meaning of your own dreams and Astral experiences rather than to rely each time upon what someone else says. Esoteric knowledge is something personal to each individual and something that an individual acquires with their own efforts.

I have not included many things of the path (the three Mountains) because they have their own process, just general things that a beginner or someone just starting the work is likely to encounter, although most things are still relevant to those who are on the path. Some of the things in the guide you will not have information about on this course, they will be made clearer by doing the Esoteric course.

Where there is a description that says something simple or general, for example "how one appears internally", you need to look at what is present in the dream and its context to get your own information on it.

Many incidents in dreams are the actions of egos or the representations/images of the mind and these need to be distinguished from situations where genuine symbols are given.

A

Age: If divine being talk about age in their places of learning in the higher dimensions, they are talking about Initiations.

Amusement Park: The illusory life of the egos.

Angel: The presence of a master.

Anger: Manifestation of the ego. You cannot pass the initiation test of fire with this.

Aeroplane: Represents how one's spiritual progress is going.

Ark: Alchemy.

Army: There are armies of the White Lodge and of the Black Lodge; the egos also form the legion. A fight against an evil army represents the legion of egos, armies of darkness, enemies, egos. If you form part of a good army look at your grade in it, it represents the level of work of the dreamer.

Authorities of the Law: If they are against the dreamer, it is Divine Justice in action, karma. In favour of the dreamer then the law protects him/her.

B

Balloons: An ordinary life, not on the path, mundane.

Banquet: A celebration of a spiritual progress.

Barriers: Obstacles and difficulties.

Bathing: In pure clean water – alchemical cleaning. In dirty water – illness.

Beard: For a man it indicates power. Any anomaly in the beard is a bad sign. In a woman, it indicates sexual degeneration.

Bicycle: How one is travelling spiritually.

Birds: In a cage means that there are elements that have come to fulfil a mission, but they are locked by the ego; with the death of the egos they are set free.

Blow (as in punching): To receive blows without a reason - attacks.

Body: Can show the state of the physical or internal bodies.

Bread: Christic atoms.

Building, A: represents where you are or where you need to reach with your spiritual work (transmutation), it is where you inhabit spiritually. A white one means purification, death of the egos.

Bull: The Masculine principle, but usually the ego.

Bullets: If someone is shooting them at you - insults directed towards you. If you are shooting them carelessly or wrongly - bad thoughts, there is a need to control the mental body.

C

Canal: The spinal column. A dry canal represents the absence of Kundalini in the spine.

Cane: The same as canal.

Car: Symbolises the inner work one is doing in the physical and shows how it is going. A couple can ride in the car when people are married, then it is related to them. Look at the type of car, its colour and condition, how you drive it, etc.

Castle: Fortress. Negative castle – stronghold of evil.

Cat: If it attacks – enemies. Black cat – black magic. On the positive side, a cat can also be related to the sexual fire.

Catastrophe: Related to the number 16. It is very bad and represents a fall or a decent.

Cave: A cavern of the mind, with all its darkness.

Century Plant (Agave Americanas, Fique plant): You are being attacked by the forces of darkness and need to protect yourself.

Chains: To break chains – to free oneself.

Chalice: The brain, the female sexual organs.

Chicken: Frightened chicken – egos of fear and weakness.

Child: A spiritual part within.

Church: A spiritual place, look at the context.

Classroom: Being taught in the internal worlds by masters, look at your behaviour in the classroom.

Cliff: Falling down a cliff symbolises an esoteric fall backwards, but it is also used in the test of air in the probative path.

Clock: Time is pressing – look at the time in terms of the sum of the numbers as stated in the topic on the meaning of numbers.

Clothes: Indicates one's spiritual state or grade; dressed in rags - spiritually bad, misery and pain. Internal bodies.

Coins: Payments for deeds, dharmic credits. Refer the number to the Kabalistic sum of the coins.

Cold (as in temperature): Solitude, sadness, bitterness.

Column: Support of the internal temple.

Combat: Fights against the egos and enemies. If it is a fight against enemies, it is a bad sign to loose. Fighting with oneself - fight against the egos.

Comet: Heralds impending disaster, you have to be careful.

Cow: The feminine principle. A white cow represents the Divine Mother, a black Cow represents her opposite.

Cross: Work with the Alchemy, sacrifices.

Crow: Negative forces threaten internally. You must protect yourself appropriately. Black magic.

D

Dagger: Assassination of the Christ, fornication.

Darkness: To be in the darkness indicates lack of consciousness in the internal worlds although it can also be due to the egos or negative entities. In the latter case, it can be cleared with the conjurations.

Dates: They should be worked out through the Kabbalistic numbers. They announce important things.

Dawn: A beginning, inspiration, a new start.

Death: If you see yourself dead, it means the death of a defect (ego) or defects. To unearth oneself - a new ego is born.

Debts: Karma is being applied to you. Karmic payments have to be made.

Defecation: Decrease of psychological defects (egos).

Dirty: A bad sign for the future. Inner filth. The danger of death for a sick person.

Disabled: To see oneself disabled or crippled - the essence is crippled. Lame - lack of sacrifice for humanity.

Desert: Aridness and solitude on the path.

Devil: Lucifer the psychological trainer, the tempter.

Doctor: Help from the Masters of Medicine in the case of illness.

Dog: There are two types of dog; the negative one steals the sexual energies, the other is a guide along the alchemical work. Dogs can also be guards.

Donkey: Inferior mental body, the ordinary mind. To ride upon it shows control of the mind.

Dove: A white dove is the Holy Spirit.

E

Eagle: The Father.

Exams: Spiritual/esoteric tests, watch how you study and prepare for them, how you sit them and the results achieved.

F

Face (one's own): How one appears internally.

Father: Representation of the eternal Father who teaches.

Flying: A certain type and level of consciousness achieved. What is seen and felt while flying needs to be interpreted. In general it is a good sign, it is even better when someone wakes up fully. However, it can be given as a help when someone is doing badly in order to give them a boost.

Fire: Gives light or destroys so it depends how it is seen.

Fisherman: Walker of the path, who spreads the teaching.

Flag: It represents success. Pay attention to the state of it.

G

Garden (pleasant): Spiritual happiness.

H

Hair (of the head): The state of one's sexual energies and spiritual state. A baldhead – lost energies.

Harvesting: The fruit of one's own deeds. If bad – there is need to learn to sow.

Hell: To be in one of the circles of the infra-dimensions. Indicates one's inner level, depending on the situation. To be unconscious there shows that the dreamer needs to work hard to eliminate the negative heavy states that drag him/or her there. It is possible to investigate there consciously, to go there to learn too. Being put into Hell is a sign of a present or future reality. To get out of there shows some success and hope.

Horse: It represents the work in the physical as a car does. To be mounted on a horse indicates spiritual advancement. If the horse is well decorated, it indicates a good sign. A runway horse is spiritually dangerous.

House: The work that one builds; built on sand for example the work has dodgy foundations and can easily fall. If it is inhabited by strangers, it shows egos.

I

Insects: Larvae. There is a need to carry out a cleaning internally; clean the Astral body with the awakened fire. Also represents attacks.

J

Jackal: Anubis judging, karma to pay.

Jewels: Depressing news. When taken out of a chest: a good sign.

Judge/Judgement: Being judged by the Masters of Karma in the internal worlds. If the judgment is in our favour, a karmic matter goes our way. If the judgment goes against us, there is a karma to pay.

K

Killing: Usually refers to the elimination of the egos, but watch who is killed, it is possible to go against the spiritual.

L

Lake: Related to sexual transmutation.

Lamb: The Son, the Christ.

Lion: Represents the law of karma. The solar man in its ascended aspect. A vicious lion represents the violent egos. Killing a fierce lion with your bare hands is triumph over certain sexual passions.

Loan: Good if it is approved and sensible, but remember that it needs to be paid. Business with the karmic law (Divine Law).

Lustful Dreams: Due to a lack of work on the egos of lust, urgent need to overcome them. Indifference in front of lust shows some chastity and balanced centres.

Lustful Odour: Lustful people emit a bad odour in the Astral.

M

Marriage: When the person is married physically and dreams of being in a married relationship with their physical partner means achievements in the alchemical transmutation, they form a true couple.

Master: Spiritual Being - will teach though not always in the way you may think, for example, if a master is in silence you have asked a silly question.

Mother: Represents the internal Divine Mother.

Mirror: How you appear in a mirror represents how you appear internally.

Money: Depends on the context, it could for example be related to greed if you are stealing it, or it could be cosmic money related to the karmic payments.

Monsters: Demons, egos. The dreamer is in the infra-dimensions, in Hell. Also a monster is faced in the test of the Guardian of the Threshold.

Moon: Represents the negative part of one's self.

Mountain: Initiation, difficulties, hard task. It is a good sign to climb one. It also means the goal.

Mud: A bad sign, a lack of death of the egos, negative influences. To get muddy – illnesses, need to eliminate egos.

N

Naked: Big troubles and/or difficulties are going to fall upon you. Look at what you go through too when naked.

Nightmares: Indicate a bad psychological state or an upset stomach. The dreamer is in the infra-dimensions.

Numbers: They are interpreted Kabalistically.

O

Owl: Can represent both wisdom and negative forces.

P

Pact: Pay careful attention if you have signed a document or made a verbal pact with anyone, because if it is done without consciousness it could have been made with the forces of darkness.

Parents: Representation of the Divine Father and Mother. To dream with parents is not necessarily a good sign; they often only appear as a last resort when the student is doing very badly. It is important to pay careful attention to what they say and do.

Path: A pathway in general means the esoteric path, initiation. If it is steep and difficult, it is the direct path of initiation. However not all are the true path. If it is a dark one, be careful. If it is in a spiral and ascending it is the path to Nirvana, without sacrifices.

Peacock: Arrogance.

Pig: Filth, laziness, fornication. There is a need to work upon oneself.

Pine: The Father.

Police: The Divine Law actively working. To be arrested - karma to pay, this is sorted out in the Tribunal of Divine Justice. Arresting someone - karma acts upon that person. You pay or they pay you for your sacrifices.

Poster: Read the information on it.

Prison cell: The law of karma acts. Psychological prison. The egos have one locked without freedom.

Punishment: Paying a karmic debt.

R

Rain: Tears, sadness and negative emotions. To walk under the rain: bitterness, pain, suffering.

Recurring dream: Something needs to be worked out.

Red beret or turban: An initiate of the Black Lodge.

Rock: Alchemical foundation of the work.

S

Scales: The Divine Law and Justice.

School: The school of life, look at the context to see how you are doing in it in relation to your esoteric work.

Sea: The sexual waters. Calm and clean - good control of the waters, chastity. Turbulent and dark - passion or lust.

Seed: An invitation or potential to be born spiritually.

Sentry: Watchful - alert consciousness. Sentry asleep - unconsciousness.

Sharks: Egos.

Shoes: How one walks along the path. Barefoot - doing badly, inadequate footwear - doing the work improperly, etc.

Snake: There are two types - the risen Kundalini and the negative tempting serpent, if the latter bites - sexual fall.

Snow: Achievements with chastity. Bad omen if the dreamer is covered in or feels cold.

Spear: Phallic symbol. Represents the work with the seminal waters.

Stairs: To go up - spiritual ascent, a beginning, new internal tasks. Being stopped on one - obstacles. Stopping on one - stagnant work. To go down is bad spiritually. To fall off is very bad. It depends of the height from which one falls.

Staff: The Kundalini, the spinal column.

Stars: Refer to what is happening in the sky.

Stigmatas: Received towards the end of the second Mountain, but if seen by someone who is not at that stage they indicate pain received while doing the spiritual work. They are very painful but you need to bear the pain somehow.

Stone: See rock.

Studying: Study in life using the esoteric work. Prepare or preparing for tests. Pay attention to the way you are studying.

Sun: The Christ. Success in initiation. Rising - something needs to be born within. Setting - something needs to die within. Dim or hazy - being obscured by egos. An eclipse of the sun - the egos eclipse and dominate the consciousness; the light is blocked; one does not allow the Being to manifest.

Swim: How one goes in the sexual waters, the waters of life. Also used for the test of water on the probative path.

Sword: The Will (willpower). Also represents the awakened Kundalini, not to be confused with a dagger.

T

Temple: A place of teachings. Also refers to the physical body in relation to it as a vessel of the being.

Thorns: Pain, voluntary suffering. Christic Will.

Tigers: They have positive and negative connotations. Positive – wisdom and intelligence. Negative – strong enemies, treason by someone, or that someone is intending to treason you. If you defeat the tiger, the danger is over.

Torch of fire: Alight - sexual fire lit/risen.

Train: The work in the physical with the vehicle/organisation that is spreading the teaching. To get off the train is to leave the teaching.

Treasure: To unbury a treasure means to recover esoteric work from the past that has been dormant.

W

War: The fight against enemies/egos.

Water: Sexual energies, transmutation. To be dragged by water indicates spiritual failure and inner weakness. It can also relate to health.

Washing one's self: A good sign if it is clean water.

Wave: Related to instability in the transmutation, look at the context.

Weapons: Used to fight evil, acquired when honours and grades are obtained. The negative side has its own weapons.

Wedding: The death of one of the participants (bride or groom). If someone dreams of himself or herself getting married, they are going to die. It may take a long or short time to manifest, but working seriously with the three keys can alter it.

Wine: Transmuted sexual energy. Generally a good sign, but not if you get drunk with it.

Worms: Larvae, decay, degeneration.

Y

Youth: Seeing yourself younger than you really are: longevity.

Week 7

Second Supplementary Topic
The Meaning of Numbers

THE MEANING OF NUMBERS

Numbers are used in the Astral world by divine beings to teach. You can therefore see them, not only when you are conscious in the Astral, but in dreams too.

Pay attention to them and use this guide to assist you in their interpretation. These numbers occur throughout the history of esotericism. They are the basis for the Tarot cards and occur throughout the work of Samael Aun Weor, the founder of modern Gnosis, and this list owes much to his work.

Many people see numbers in their dreams, so this guide will be useful; it is just a summary of the numbers and a short guide rather than a complete description. Each number needs to be interpreted according to the context of the experience and the spiritual work the person is doing. Bear in mind that many of the terms used are esoteric; they apply especially to those who have taken up the spiritual path and are beyond the scope of this course to explain. I have other courses such as the Esoteric one, where I explain the knowledge of the inner worlds and the spiritual path more fully.

The numbers go from 1 to 22. If a number is over 22, you add up its parts, so for example if you have 23 you add $2 + 3$ giving the number 5.

When numbers within the same type of item have been given you add them up together, so for example you get $24.48, it breaks down as $2 + 4 + 4 + 8 = 18$.

When separate numbers of completely different types of items have been given you add them up separately and then get the meaning of each separate number, for example: 23 stones and 57 footballs breaks down as $2 + 3 = 5$ and $5 + 7 = 12$. So you need to look at the meaning of the numbers 5 and 12.

When you are summing up a series of related numbers such as day, year and month in a birthday, you treat them separately but you sum up to a maximum of 9 for each sub total. You only go over 9 when you add up for the final total. So for example, 11/12/1995 breaks down as: $1 + 1 = 2$, $1 + 2 = 3$, $1 + 9 + 9 + 5 = 24$; $2 + 4 = 6$; the total then will be $2 + 3 + 6 = 11$, because in this case you don't go over the number 9 in a sub total you break the 24 down 2 + 4 = 6. Then add up the sub totals, 2 + 3 + 6 = 11.

You only go as far as 12 when summing up hours of the day, so for example, don't use 21:00 hours but 9:00 hours whether it is the morning or the night.

THE NUMBERS

Number 1   The Magician.

It represents the masculine principle, the wisdom of the Father and the Unity.

It also represents something that begins, (every beginning is difficult and you have to sow to be able to reap).

It also represents the sword, which is willpower and power (that power is the power to awaken and to dominate the passions of the egos).

The 1 unfolds to become 2. The Unity is the root of the Duality, the Father unfolds into the Mother.

Number 2   The Priestess.

The Wife of the Magician, the receptive Feminine principle.

This is a favourable number.

"The wind and the waves always favour the one who knows how to navigate" (the waves are Alchemical).

The two columns of the temple.

Number 3   The Empress.

The Divine Mother.

Spiritual and material success and productivity, overcoming obstacles.

The 1 and 2 unfold to produce 3.

Number 4   The Emperor.

Ruling, progress, success and mercy.

It also represents stability; establish a solid base in order to succeed.

The cubic stone which is the basis of the spiritual work must be carved.

Number 5 The Hierarch.

The divine law, Karma, this includes the persons karma.

It is also Mars, which is a rigorous spiritual war.

The five pointed star, the solar man must be born. Fight so that the star can point upwards.

Number 6 Indecision.

The choice between different paths.

It is also temptation - the struggle between love and desire. The lover.

In triumph - victory, good luck, in failure - Erotic violation

Number 7 Triumph.

The Chariot of War.

Wars, struggles, battle, difficulties, penitence, pain and bitterness.

One must learn to use the Staff and the Sword and will thus achieve great victory. (Willpower is vital).

Number 8 Justice.

It signifies hard tests suffering and pain.

Within it are to be found Initiatic tests and the work of Job, who had enormous patience and who suffered much.

It is also righteousness, justice, and equilibrium. Seek the good, cost what it may. Fulfil the law with good actions.

Number 9 The Hermit.

Initiation, solitude and suffering.

The number 9 also represents the Ninth Sphere, the work with sex. There is great suffering in the Ninth Sphere so one must learn to understand, to suffer and to be resigned; those who do not will fail.

Number 10 Retribution.

The wheel of fortune, successful dealings, changes.

It is also the Wheel of Samsara, the tragic wheel which is the law of return.

It promises good and bad fortune, ascents and descents, and circumstances which repeat in a different form.

Number 11 Persuasion.

The tame Lion, the divine law is in your favour.

Have no Fear.

Mars.

The work with the Fire, with the force of love.

Persuasion has more power than violence, a soft word pacifies anger. Persuasion is in essence, a subtle, spiritual force.

Number 12 The Disciple.

It implies sacrifices and sufferings, tests and pain.

Alchemy is vital to take the pain away.

Number 13 Immortality.

Death and resurrection, transformations; it indicates total change.

But death has two aspects, the human physical death and the inner death of the egos.

It can also signify something new.

Number 14 Temperance.

It is chastity, transmutation, the waters. One must work hard, chiselling the Stone, without which one cannot achieve sexual transmutation.

Matrimonial association, long life, stability, no change.

Number 15 Passion.

It warns of Danger. Failure in love.

It is the work with the tempter, which esoterically is called Satan or the Devil, in the process of dissolution of the egos.

The passion is based in the Luciferic Fire - the main defect is sexual passion, lust.

Number 16 Fragility.

The fallen tower; the terrible fall of the initiate.

It brings punishment.

Avoid this date.

Number 17 Hope.

Sex under the control of the Spirit.

Number 18 Twilight.

Hidden Enemies - they can appear at any moment and can be physical or internal.

Illnesses.

Bad for business.

Number 19 Inspiration.

The radiant sun, successes, good luck. It promises total Victory, be it through one's own efforts or with the help of other people.

It also can refer to working with the Philosophical Stone.

Number 20 Resurrection.

The resurrection of the dead (from the death of the egos comes life, the resurrection of the soul is only possible through initiation. Human beings are spiritually dead and can only resuscitate by means of Initiation).

Favourable changes, take advantage of them. Put an end to weaknesses.

Number 21   Foolishness or Transmutation.

The Fool: failure, committing folly in the spiritual work.

Transmutation: It indicates that you must transmute.

Number 22   The crown of life.

The return to the light, the incarnation of truth within.

Triumph, everything turns out well, power, strength, good fortune.

ADDITIONAL INFORMATION ABOUT CLOCKS

When a clock is shown, the hour is of great importance. A clock signifies that time is pressing so you need to see the hour. These hours have their own meaning that is different from the other numbers. These numbers refer only to those shown in a clock, although the hours are related to the numbers. The first hour is related to the number 10 and each number goes in that sequence right through to the hour 12, which relates to the number 21. The hour 13 relates to the number 22.

Below is what Samael Aun Weor has written about them:

> **1st Hour:** The transcendental study of Occultism.
>
> **2nd Hour:** Persuasion has more power than violence.
>
> **3rd Hour:** Serpents, dogs and fire. Work with the kundalini.
>
> **4th Hour:** The beginner will wander at night amongst graves, he will suffer the horrors of the visions; he will surrender to Magic and Goecy (he will be attacked in the astral by millions of black magicians) all this is to move him away from the Path.
>
> **5th Hour:** Superior waters from heaven. The disciple learns to be chaste and understands the value of the seminal fluid.
>
> **6th Hour:** Keep still, immobile. The test of the Guardian of the Threshold; courage is needed to defeat him.

7th Hour: The fire comforts the inanimate beings, and if the priest or purified man steals it and projects, if he mixes it in holy oil and consecrates it, he will manage to cure the illnesses by applying it to the affected parts. The initiate sees here his financial fortune threatened and his business fail.

8th Hour: The astral virtues of the elements of the seeds of every kind.

9th Hour: Nothing has ended yet. The initiate increases his vision towards the limits of the intangible world. He arrives to the infinite threshold. The divine light reveals and new dangers appear.

10th Hour: The doors of Heaven open and the man comes out of his lethargy. This is the second initiation of the Major Mysteries and the initiate travels in his Etheric Body. It is the wisdom of John the Baptist.

11th Hour: Angels, cherubims and seraphims fly; there is joy in the sky. The earth awakens and the sun arises from Adam. This belongs to the Great Initiations of the Major Mysteries where only the terror of the Law reigns.

12th Hour: The towers of fire are disturbed. This is the triumphal entry of the Master in the happiness of Nirvana or his renunciation of it for the love of Humanity, which leads him to be a Bodhisattva of Compassion.

Week 8

Overcoming Obstacles

There are many obstacles to overcome when learning about Astral projection and having almost any Astral experience. Most people don't work to overcome the obstacles, but those who do, find success. Every obstacle needs to be seen and overcome if that is possible.

This may involve sacrifices and big efforts, but rather than falling down its better to see what the obstacles are, to persist and to overcome them, then you get not only experience but also strength and willpower that will help you in your life.

What sometimes seems like an insurmountable obstacle may be overcome with patience, effort and further esoteric work. You need to see the particular obstacles that you face in order to overcome them. I am going to mention some of the common problems that can be overcome if you are willing to put some work into it. In life nothing is given for free; everything costs and some of these costs are paid in effort, time and determination. These are just a few examples; problems of all kinds arise in so many different ways, again and again and it is important to keep track of your main goal and to work to overcome them, within whatever limitations you may or may not have.

PROBLEMS WITH LAZINESS

Laziness can be a very big obstacle in astral projection. It is a problem not only for astral projection but also for the spiritual work as a whole.

Laziness in itself is an ego (refer to the Self Knowledge course for information on these), besides doing the general work upon the egos you also need to go against laziness by doing something even when you don't feel like doing it. If you don't do this, you will always stay trapped within those feelings that laziness brings. If you do the activity that laziness is trying to stop you from doing, you will gain inner strength and willpower.

Sometimes it is difficult to spot. It can hide itself behind very nice excuses, which can sound convincing at times and one likes to hear and go along with, but do not be deceived by them - it is just the way that laziness operates in order to trick someone.

Many people find that at the beginning of the course laziness is not there so much, because they are eager to try something new. The eagerness continues if they see things happening and working. However, when things stop happening, the morale goes down and one begins to slow down, you begin to listen to those excuses more and more and laziness and entropy begins to settle. In this situation, it is easy to forget what you need to do and eventually you may even consider giving it up.

Not only the body but also the mind is controlled by the ego of laziness. Therefore, you literally need to make yourself practice your exercises. For example, go to your room or sit down/lay down where you normally do your exercise and do it. If you have let the momentum slip and are out of practice, get back into it gradually so that you re-educate yourself. Start with an exercise for a very short period of time - up to 10 minutes, but no more. If you do it any longer when you are starting back, the difficulties that you may face can mean that you may create an additional resistance to the exercises. So get back into it gradually but methodically.

By doing this, you will bring back the mode and momentum of doing the exercises. Eventually you begin to see a light at the end of the tunnel and you gradually regain the work.

BEING DISHEARTENED

There is big difference between reading and talking about Astral projection and actually doing it yourself. Sometimes expectations are different to reality and one discovers that it takes a lot more work to Astral project than one had thought, perhaps because it sounded so simple yet proved difficult to do.

It is very easy then to become disheartened, to think that you cannot do it and then to consider giving up.

It is important to realise that it is something that has to be learned - just like any new skill - and that is why you need to "practice the exercises" because it is a process of learning. You are unlikely to Astral project as soon as you have the techniques and, even if you do, repeat success takes much work and maintaining it even more. The exercises are given so that you learn with patience how to do them. Learning any new skill takes time and effort.

Therefore, you do need to put work into it, a consistent daily effort, which makes all the difference. More importantly, when you try your exercises, don't expect too much at all, simply do them in order to practice your exercises again with the aim of really being good at it.

It is important to get into a routine and begin to build up just as it is done in sports. No one becomes good at sports overnight; neither would someone who has been away from training be good at it overnight. They need to go back into it, training gradually again until they reach to the point where they left and improve from there.

If the consistency is there, you become good at it; because you learn how it works and you gradually know the way you behave psychologically and physically when you are trying the exercises.

Problems at home, at work or even a visit somewhere for a period of time, can sometimes throw your routine out of the window, so efforts need to be made to get back into the routine of practice again and again.

PROBLEMS WITH PAIN WHEN DOING EXERCISES

Feeling pain can be enough to stop the exercise of Astral projection. Pain can commonly arise when trying to project when one overdoes it, when one is recovering from an illness or when one is not used to the exercises.

When the body feels pain, it automatically withdraws from the cause of pain, so you will sometimes feel negative towards the exercises if you have pushed yourself or forced your body to go through pain when trying them.

Therefore, you must not push the body to the point of pain. The body and the mind must be trained gently and gradually to do the exercises. The capacity of endurance of the physical body varies from person to person, after an illness, the body is even more sensitive to pain and discomfort, and therefore greater care should be taken. When the body has gone through an illness, the body will not take long to get tired or feel pain. The best thing then is to try the exercises for very short periods of time, according to what the body can tolerate, before it becomes painful or uncomfortable.

After an illness, it would be best to start with very short relaxation exercises and then, if you are able you increase the time each day until you feel ready to practise the Astral (but never force the body) see what you can take and do not push it; gradually build it up.

If you are simply trying to go back into the exercises because you have drifted away from them and you feel pain when you to the exercises, the approach is similar. However, it will take less time to get back into the exercises since the body only has to be trained to remain still in a position for a while. At the same time, the mind will need to go back to the discipline of focusing on the exercises.

The main thing in both cases is to get started in the exercises, gradually going further each time. If you persist, you will eventually wake in your dreams and/or experience Astral projection. Once that happens, carry on with your daily exercises, maintaining and increasing them.

Like most things, these exercises improve with practice, so it is important to be continuous and consistent with them. This also implies patience and lots of it is needed, since we have to re-educate ourselves out of old patterns of behaviour into new ones - this takes time and effort to do. When the continuity in the exercises for whatever reason is lost, it needs to be built back up again.

You also have to watch that you don't force yourself, increase the time spent practicing gradually, so that you get used to it and stop if you feel you are forcing something or if the body rebels and feels uncomfortable with it.

LACK OF THE ABILITY TO CONCENTRATE

Although I have given the techniques to actually project as examples in this topic, concentrating upon what you are doing throughout the day is a vital part of the routine for Astral projection, and any routine that you have must include working towards concentrating and being aware of what you are doing throughout the day. If this is not done, the mind will never be properly trained or educated to be on what you are doing, and even the best techniques of projection are not very effective unless you do it.

When you do your exercise to project and the mind keeps thinking about other things, it is due to a lack of practice of being concentrated during the day and of daily practices of the concentration/visualisation exercises.

The latter can be incorporated into your daily routine quite easily, but it takes a great deal of willpower to concentrate and be aware of what you are doing through a whole day. Most people do not even attempt it, but it can be done. It also seemed impossible to me once, but I managed to do it after much effort. It helps a great deal to have the information about psychology from the Self Knowledge and Esoteric courses, because when we try to concentrate, we deal with the different states of mind and these (what we call egos) are the obstacles to concentration and awareness. However, put simply, if you put in all your willpower and make the maximum effort to do it, you will achieve it and then you can really project.

~

SUMMARY OF THE COURSE EXERCISES

I am going to list the various techniques that we have used on this course so that you have a record of them all together in one place, but refer back to the original topic for information on it. There is one more new technique to Astral project with at the end of this list; it involves watching the dream images as you go to sleep.

Here is a list of the exercises on the course:

1. Awareness/concentration on activities
2. Relaxation
3. Remembering dreams
4. Daily concentration/visualisation exercise (10 minutes and more)
5. Waking up in dreams
6. The Conjurations and the Circle of Protection
7. Concentration on the heart

8. Mantras
9. Projecting to a room
10. Projecting to a place
11. Watching the dream images (in this topic)

Continue to read over and practise them after this course has finished and build on them so that they become useful tools for your search. Work out a daily and weekly program for yourself from the exercises given and stick to it. Maintain the awareness/concentration on activities, remembering dreams, the daily concentration exercise (10 minutes and more), jumping and pulling the finger and the conjurations and circle of protection every day. These are important to keep going with.

FINAL EXERCISE OF THE COURSE

Here is another technique to Astral project with:

Watching the Dream Images
Relax the body as normal, lying on your back if you are comfortable like that, and then keep relaxing into the sleep. Watch for the first dream images and then get up slowly from bed, if you catch it at the right moment you will get up in the Astral.

You have to watch that you don't miss the opportunity and fall asleep instead; it takes a bit of practice. These dream images are different from thoughts, they appear to be almost real and you will know them when you experienced them, if you have not done so already.

There is a variation on this exercise, which is to go back into a dream. When you wake up, if you remember the dream you can go back into it - this is useful if you want to get more information on something. You just remember the dream and place yourself in it using your imagination; if you really place yourself in it and sleep arrives, you will find yourself back in that dream.

CONCLUSION

This course has provided an outline of the Astral and provided exercises that lay a solid foundation for experience. There is much more to learn and subsequent courses will give more information in depth. So that you have the tools and information for your own search into the hidden esoteric side of life and become a true investigator of the reality that exists, not only of what can be perceived with the five senses but beyond it.

Where to go from Here

This is the final topic of the Astral course, but although it is the last, it is really just the beginning.

It is one thing to get into the Astral plane, but another to be an esotericist. Anyone can fly and explore the Astral world, but few penetrate its secrets.

To do that, much more information about what is there is required. You will find this on the Self Knowledge and Esoteric courses.

Many people are no doubt content to dabble and experiment here and there, and will move on from this course to other Astral methods and courses given elsewhere. Others will want to explore deeper into the nature of themselves and life and it is these latter people that may one day be the walkers of the esoteric path in the future.

I have given only a tiny amount of what I know about the higher and lower realms on this course. There is only so much information that can be given, practiced and understood in an eight week course - after this there is so much more to learn. The Astral is a way to get knowledge, but if you don't change and walk along the esoteric path, you will never get real knowledge or wisdom, you will only get the basic end, which is usually inaccurate information and you will have to muddle your way through a complex web of experiences that you have no way of understanding.

As well as continuing with the courses, I shall outline some things you can do so that you can continue your Astral exploration and practice in an effective way in the future. It is worth looking at what you have achieved in this eight-week period, as what you have achieved will be largely due to the efforts you made in it.

There is much more to learn and do, so this is not the end of the attempts that can be made on these courses to get into the Astral, rather, it is just the beginning. This course laid the foundation for the exploration of the Astral, but future courses will give information about the bigger picture of what is there. On these courses you will be able to practice and use what you have learnt on this one to explore and discover the nature both of yourself and of the scheme of things in life.

Then, you will become better equipped as an investigator and searcher into reality. When looking back it is very easy to see how things could have been done better, so have a look at the mistakes you made, times when you didn't try, did something else, didn't follow the program and so on.

Resolve to correct whatever mistakes you have found when you start the next course and keep looking for and correcting mistakes, because if you do this, you will be able to make real improvements and will be able to advance in your esoteric search.

We are going to look at setting routines and overcoming obstacles in this topic so that you can create an effective order in your Astral exercises and create a foundation for the future.

PLANNING THE EXERCISES AND YOUR ASTRAL STRATEGY

Planning and organising your time and activities is very important. If you want the Astral to work, you will have to make a special effort now that the Astral course is over, so that you plan what you are going to do ahead and stick to it. If you do not keep to your program you will find that the Astral easily falls away, it takes a lot of effort to build up and not much to lose it. Additionally, the events that take place every day have a way of taking one's attention away from the esoteric work, so you need to be very disciplined in order to keep going and to achieve your goals in the Astral.

Make use of every event in life to learn from yourself and to carry out the esoteric work, learn to use each moment, build up the esoteric work that you do, so that it is the main centre of your focus, drive and interest. Live each day like this and your life will be radically transformed.

Work out in a diary (get one if you do not have one) a structure for your daily exercises. You can plan for the week ahead, work out the times that you are going to spend doing them and work out which ones you will do.

In this way, you become organised and you know what you are going to do and whether or not you have done it.

This of course does not stop you from taking any opportunity that you might have during the day to use to practice any of the exercises.

GETTING INTO A MODE OF PRACTICING

It is very easy to lose track of the exercises and to feel that the experience of Astral projection has slipped away from you. To make it work again you have to get back into the mode of practising, to re-evaluate what you have done and what you are doing and to draw up a new plan.

If you draw up a new plan, try to stick to it because the results make it worth it. When one is caught up in the identification with daily activities, with the job, with friends, with family and so on, the esoteric work slips away and its importance is easily forgotten or pushed to one side. However, that does not mean that it actually has lost its importance, it is just that the individual does not see it any more. It is far more important than you can imagine and, when this life is over, it was all that really mattered. Time that is wasted is never recovered again.

DEDICATION AND DISCIPLINE

It is possible to have Astral experiences here and there when trying to project but for the Astral to work with any regularity one must be completely dedicated to it. To be able to project whenever you want to requires a very strong effort throughout each day and this means being disciplined and orderly, staying focused upon the esoteric work, no matter what you are doing.

Discipline in relation to the physical body is also very important for Astral projection, since the body and the mind need to get used to a different way of approaching sleep. It is up to each person to set up their own routine and to be as disciplined, or not, as they wish. I am explaining from my experience how to get the best results and many others who have tried the exercises on this course have confirmed that what I am saying here in this topic applies. It takes a lot of effort and willpower, but it does pay off.

If you continue with further courses, always maintain your Astral exercises. They will be the means with which you can investigate, experience and prove what is written in them and will allow you to acquire your own esoteric knowledge - far beyond what you can read in any book. The experiences you get will always be remembered and they will help you to get through the difficult times of life and the esoteric path, thus building the foundation of a faith that derives from knowledge and direct experience - something that very few people have.

∼

Index

A

Akashic records 13
Alchemy 8, 55, 119
Anubis 13, 127
Awareness 23, 30, 31, 35, 47, 52, 53, 54, 81, 82, 87

B

Bellilin 93, 98
Bodhisattva 106, 140

C

Century plant 91, 104, 124
Circle of protection 95
Concentration 15, 24, 32, 79, 85
Conjuration 14, 17, 18, 22, 46, 61, 63, 76, 86, 92, 125
Consciousness 5, 14, 30, 55, 81, 118

D

Darkness 14, 102, 105, 119, 124, 125, 129
Death 2, 7, 16, 18, 62, 76, 120, 125, 129, 132
Demon 90, 112, 128
Divine father 129
Divine mother 112, 128
Dream symbols 121
Dreams 3
Drugs 14, 54

E

Egos 4, 18, 30, 80, 90, 91
Esoteric path 13, 29, 91, 103, 106, 110, 112, 113, 114, 129, 150, 153
Evil 90, 92, 113

F

Falling asleep 82
Father 96, 112, 126, 129, 135
Fear 15, 17, 23, 26, 35, 37, 43, 46, 47, 48, 55, 63, 76, 77, 101, 102, 124

G

Guides 13

H

Heart 33, 73, 74, 76, 80, 85, 86, 87

I

Illness 119, 123, 126, 129, 138, 140, 144
Infra-dimensions 127
Intuition 8, 21, 110

J

Jupiter 93, 100, 105

K

Karma 123, 125, 127, 128, 136

L

Laziness 37, 129, 142
Lucid dreaming 12, 18, 52, 57, 60

M

Mantra 11, 65
Master 57, 91, 99, 107, 123, 124, 126, 127, 128
Masters 3
Mental plane 54, 90

N

Negative entities 90, 125
Nightmares 21, 47, 90, 129

O

Obstacles 141

P

Pain 125, 130, 131, 136, 144
Polyvision 13, 14
Projection to a room 114
Psyche 3, 31
Psychology 10, 146

R

Rabolu 54, 91
Relaxation 10, 38, 39, 40, 42, 47, 63, 74, 144
Remembering dreams 11

S

Science 5
Self knowledge 5, 22, 87, 99, 103, 111, 113, 142, 146, 150
Silver cord 3, 28, 34
Spiritual beings 3, 7, 26, 46, 90, 94, 112, 114
Subconscious 3, 5, 17, 20, 23, 25, 31, 52, 99, 105, 111
Symbols 8, 111, 121

T

Teachings 2, 113, 131
Travelling 113

V

Vibrations 85, 86
Visualisation 32, 49

W

Waking up in dreams 52

Book Order Information

For order options visit:
http://www.absolutepublishing.net

Online Course Information

To register for the free online course in Astral Travel visit:
http://www.gnosticweb.org

Other courses written by V.M. Beelzebub include Self Knowledge and Esoteric Wisdom. All courses can be undertaken online free of charge. The Esoteric course is only available after the Astral and Self Knowledge courses have been completed.

Live Courses

Live courses are available in Australia, United States and Canada. For upcoming course information email: course@gnosticweb.org or visit http://www.gnosticweb.org